YOUNG EMMA

LIBRARY OF WALES

William Henry Davies was born in a pub in 1871, and learnt early in life to rely on his wits and his fists and to drink. As a young man his restless spirit of adventure led him to set off for America, and he worked around the country taking casual jobs where he could, thieving and begging where he couldn't. His experiences and adventures were both dramatic and harrowing – he was thrown into prison in Michigan, beaten up in New Orleans, witnessed a lynching in Tennessee, and got drunk pretty well everywhere – and were later documented in his hugely successful *Autobiography of a Super-Tramp*, published in 1908. After returning to Britain permanently following an accident which cost him a leg, he lived a frugal existence in London and began to write poetry, producing at his own expense a volume entitled *The Soul's Destroyer, and Other Poems* (1905). Following the acclaim of Super-Tramp, which was championed by George Bernard Shaw and Edward Thomas, he published numerous further collections of verse, including *Nature Poems and Others* (1908), *Farewell to Poesy* (1909) and *Songs of Joy* (1911). Despite his fame within literary circles, he preferred to lead a reclusive life, and did not marry until he was over fifty – a journey documented in the manuscript of *Young Emma,* which he had asked to be destroyed but which was published posthumously in 1980 after being discovered in the safe of the publisher Jonathan Cape. He died in 1940.

YOUNG EMMA

W. H. DAVIES

Parthian, Cardigan SA43 1ED
www.parthianbooks.com
The Library of Wales is a Welsh Government initiative which
highlights and celebrates Wales' literary heritage in the English language.
Published with the financial support of the Welsh Books Council.
www.thelibraryofwales.com
Series Editor: Dai Smith
First published in 1980
Library of Wales edition first published 2015©
Foreword © C.V. Wedgewood
ISBN 9781910409459
Cover image: *Yvonne*,
Walter Richard Sickert (1860-1942)
Private Collection / Photo © Christie's Images / Bridgeman Images
Cover design: Marc Jennings
Typeset by Elaine Sharples
Printed and bound by Dinefwr Press, Llandybie, Wales

FOREWORD
BY C. V. WEDGWOOD

In August 1924 the poet W. H. Davies, who first made his mark as a writer with his *Autobiography of a Super Tramp*, wrote to his publisher Jonathan Cape, 'I want to discuss a new book I am writing. Another human document; so much so that it will have to be published under the name "Anonymous".' Six weeks later he wrote, 'I am sending you *Young Emma*. It frightens me now it is done.'

The book was autobiographical – the story of his recent marriage to a girl he had picked up one evening at a bus stop. She was not yet a prostitute but would probably have ended that way if she had not met him. Emma was a country girl who had come to London, become pregnant by a man whom she could not marry, was without resources and afraid to go back to her people.

Davies knew nothing of her story when he took her home. He was over fifty and looking for a wife. He did not even realise that she was pregnant until she gave birth prematurely to a child which did not survive. His account of the frantic quest for a hospital that would take her through seven long hours of a pitch dark night has the anguish of a nightmare.

Meanwhile he believed he had contracted a venereal disease and thought that young Emma was to blame. But by that time he was in love with her – and no wonder, for she was affectionate, grateful, cheerful, good-natured, pretty and a natural home-maker. They moved to the country and started a new life together. Emma became his wife and all ended well.

The relationship between them, as he describes it, is wholly convincing and the portrait of the girl is extraordinarily vivid and sympathetic. William Plomer wrote, in a later report on the book: 'It reads as if nothing in it was invented and yet the effect is that of a short novel very skilfully written with a happy ending.'

Plomer's report was written in 1972 when the tastes of the reading public had greatly altered. When Jonathan Cape first received the book, in 1924, he feared that its publication might damage Davies's reputation. He consulted Bernard Shaw, who had written the preface to *The Autobiography of a Super-Tramp*. In a letter about the book Shaw called *Young Emma* an 'amazing document' but agreed with Jonathan that its publication might do harm to Davies; also, what right had he to give away his wife? 'If they were both dead it would be another matter: I am always in favour of publishing genuine documents.'*

Davies had by now, belatedly, said something about the book to his wife. 'She is very much alarmed at it,' he wrote to Jonathan, '*As she is only 24 years of age and has every prospect of outliving us all* I have come to the conclusion that the MS. must be destroyed and not get into the hands of strangers in about 50 years' time from now. So will you please return the MS. and let me have a note to say you have destroyed the two type-written copies? There are a few passages in it that I can use in poems and prose sketches. As the matter now stands, my mind can never be at rest. Please don't try to persuade me to do anything different, as a book that is not fit to be published now can never be fit.'

It may seem strange, to say the least of it, that Davies had waited so long to tell his wife about the book. But it is very clear from his account of 'young Emma' that the whole business of writing was a mystery to her which she looked upon with awe as something quite beyond her understanding. We know that, later, he read his poems to her and indeed wrote many of them to her, but this was a different matter from discussing a prose work in progress.

* The letter from George Bernard Shaw to Jonathan Cape, dated November 1924, is published as an appendix to this book.

Jonathan Cape answered Davies's letter a few days later: 'I am sending you under registered post your original MS. as you request. I have not destroyed the two copies as yet but I will do so next week. I have delayed replying and I have also delayed the destruction of the two copies in case you might on reflection feel that to destroy everything is a little too drastic.'

To this Davies replied a week later: 'Many thanks for the original MS. I have already begun to make use of some of the material, and you can destroy the two type-written copies as soon as you like.' He then went on to discuss other publishing business, and does not appear at any later time to have made further enquiry as to the destruction of the two typescripts. They were not in fact destroyed but put carefully away in a safe.

Davies died in 1940. Two years later, when I was working as a reader, Jonathan Cape came into my room one morning with a mysterious air, placed a typescript on my desk and said, 'Tell me what you think of that.' He did not tell me who had written it until I had almost finished my reading.

Though I knew and admired the poems of W. H. Davies I had not at that time read the *Super-Tramp* and his prose style was unfamiliar to me. But I was struck at once by the direct and unconventional manner of the writing and the skill with which the narrative was unfolded. The picture of the streets at night and the atmosphere of London in the immediate aftermath of the First World War made it a lively social document as well as a valuable personal record – and a good short novel too. But Mrs Davies was alive and still in her early forties. While she lived publication was out of the question.

Nothing further happened for many years. Jonathan died in 1960. By then I had left the office, and I have an impression that he and I were the only people who knew about the typescript – and I had almost forgotten it. Then, in 1972, during the rearrangement and sorting of old files, my report on *Young Emma* came to light, aroused interest and led to a search for the typescripts, which were discovered soon after at the back of a safe.

Catherine Storr and William Plomer then read and reported on the book, both in very favourable terms.

'It can be read with pleasure for its own sake, and is of course valuable as an addition to Davies's printed accounts of his life and character,' wrote William Plomer, and went on to discuss the ethics of preserving and publishing it:

> The case for preserving it is obvious, but it could be thought that there is a case for destroying it. Why? Because Davies wished it to be destroyed. His main reason was that his wife might still be alive in fifty years' time – i.e. from 1924. Apparently he was right, and she may still be alive in two years' time, or long after that.
>
> She presumably has no idea that the book has *not* been destroyed. If she knew that it exists still, she would almost certainly wish it to be destroyed.
>
> So to preserve it, as Jonathan Cape did, and as we are doing, is to go against Davies's wishes and Mrs Davies's wishes.
>
> I find it difficult to imagine that any intelligent person with literary knowledge or discrimination could, after reading this book, be so high-minded as to destroy it or to recommend it to be destroyed. It would seem a form of vandalism.
>
> The truth is that if authors of repute wish their unpublished writings to be destroyed, they should destroy them themselves.

He concluded that the book must be preserved but must await publication until after the death of its heroine.

His verdict, that writers who wish their books to be destroyed must do it themselves, recalled a suspicion which had crossed my mind when I first saw the correspondence between Davies and Jonathan. Very few authors truly wish to see their work destroyed. Did Davies deceive himself? Did he half-consciously hope that a copy might survive? There is something about the wording of his last request to Jonathan – 'You can destroy [the typescripts] as soon as you like' – which is noticeably weaker than his first request, and even that is a little ambiguous – 'Let me have a note to say that you have destroyed the two typewritten copies.' I am not ascribing insincerity to Davies, only an unspoken, unadmitted desire to reprieve his work. There is indeed a depth of meaning in William Plomer's dictum that authors who wish to do away with their unpublished writings should destroy them themselves.

The book was preserved, but publication was postponed while Mrs Davies lived. On both counts I feel that this was the right decision: right to plan publication and right to wait until after the death of Mrs Davies. She died in 1979.

I felt this all the more when I re-read the book early in 1980. With greater understanding and experience than I had had nearly forty years before, I found it even more vivid, interesting and moving.

Why should English literature be deprived of so delightful a character as young Emma? And how could anyone wish to cause distress to the old lady who in her youth had been young Emma?

YOUNG EMMA

W. H. DAVIES

INTRODUCTION

THIS BOOK is a human document, and I will take it as a kindness if it is allowed to remain anonymous, and no one seeks to know the name of its author. Not that I have any concern about my own self; but when I bring others into the story of this strange life, where I have not shrunk from self-revelation, it is a different matter. The name I have made for myself as a writer – which I have always taken less seriously than others have taken it – will look after me in the end. If my work lives, it will be strong enough to look after my character; and if it dies when my body dies, farewell to them both – both work and character must be forgotten, and that's the end of me and all my belongings.

Although the work may be praised for its style and language, I would not like anyone to think or say that the matter itself is foul; and that the force of a natural genius has made common ditchwater sing like a pure spring. For had I not been convinced that the book was pure, in spite of the matter it deals with, it would never have been written or published.

As the early part of my life is already known, I begin this new one in my fiftieth year. It is not usual for a man to begin writing a second life, after he has lived for more than half a century, but the matter in this book will justify it, I think. For even though this new life is still no more than two years old, it seems to be much greater than the longer life that is past, because of its greater intensity. Let us judge it then, not by its number of breaths, but by the number of times that breath is held or lost, either under a deep emotion caused by love, or when we stand before an object of interest or beauty.

We will now come to the great matter in hand; how I decided, about two years ago, to change my way of living, and how it was done. At that time I was living in a small room, poorly furnished, in the West End of London. But my position was not to be judged by that for, although I was far from being rich, I was still rich enough to live in a better place and with more comfort. One reason for living in that squalid place was the great difficulty of getting another, owing to the shortage of houses, being the result of the Great War. But even if this were not the case, it is hardly likely that I would have taken the trouble to move. For I had made up my mind to find a woman to share my life; one who would leave London altogether, and go with me into the green country, and be satisfied. I was beginning to find Society a pest, and common friendship unsatisfactory. I began to see that, although people liked me personally, their interest in me would only last as long as my power to keep my name before the public. So, to save future trouble and inconvenience, I decided to give them up, before their time came to sacrifice me. It was with bitter feeling that I used to think, when sitting alone at night, that I had scores of people to follow me in the sun, but not one to follow me into the shade – unless Fame had brought me Fortune too, which it certainly had not.

But in searching for a wife, I found it no easy matter to get one to my liking. One woman, whom I thought would make a good wife refused me on account of blood-relationship. Another, who had a great admiration for my work, and liked me personally, could not make up her mind to trust her life with mine: for, said she – 'your joy is self-contained, and I am very much afraid you would be none the happier for being a married man.'

Strange to say, there were two other women of a different opinion, whom I could have married at any time, but whom I did not like well enough. If they had not shown their liking for me so plainly, most likely I would have liked them better; for I had never yet met a woman that I really disliked. One of these two women was an actress, but I knew that there could be no union between the footlights and a quiet study. The other was rich, and that would not do either; for I wanted a woman who was worth working for, and would be dependent on my own loving kindness.

Perhaps it would interest my readers to know, at this part of my narrative, what the author of it looks like personally. I have already said that I am over fifty years of age, but I have not said that I could pass for a much younger man. Judged by my fellow men, I am small and insignificant, but even the biggest men have been impressed by my strong face; a good, straightforward eye, and, for a small man, an unusual breadth of shoulder. 'You are ugly enough to please any woman,' said one of my lady friends – 'no matter how particular she might be.'

My moral courage is not very great, but my physical courage has been tested on several occasions. For instance, if I heard anyone breaking into my house at night, I would certainly not make a noise to drive him away; but would dress quietly, with the intention of seeing what kind of man he was, and coming into personal contact with his body. At one time I was disturbed at night by several young fellows, who had taken rooms above my own. The first night I did not know what to do, for did not know whether they were trying to rob me of my sleep, with intention, or were only naturally noisy with youth. When I put the matter before them, the next morning, they, with the oily tongues of well-bred gentlemen, assured me that they meant no harm, and made no noise at all. 'Perhaps you heard mice,' said one of them. 'Well,' I answered – 'if the mice in this house are big enough to shake the walls and floors, I must certainly kill one or two of them.' The second night the noises were worse, as I had expected; for there are no people more daring than cowards, when they are in numbers. But when they began their devildom, on the third night, a strange happiness came over me, for I knew that the time had come for action. I never felt so calm in all my life; and, while I was dressing, I was actually humming a tune. But they must have heard me coming, for, when I got upstairs on their landing, and knocked at their door, they made no answer, and pretended to be asleep. However, I knocked again, and then heard a voice – 'Who's there?'

'Open the door,' I answered, quietly.

'What do you want?' asked the same voice.

'I will let you know when the door is opened,' I said; 'I don't know how many of you are here, neither do I care.'

However, they would not open the door, but said they would see me the next morning.

'Nothing is more certain than our meeting in the morning,' I said.

When the morning came, I waited for them, with my door wide open, so that I might hear them coming down the stairs. As they had not come downstairs by nine o'clock, I decided to go out and fetch some milk, which would take me no more than two minutes. But it was in that short time that they all came down, four of them, I believe, and disappeared, and I have never seen or heard of them since. I have always been sorry that those young cowards escaped punishment, and yet it was probably well for me that they did. For that same morning, I had gone into a back room to split a log. The log was so hard and knotty that I had had it for a long time, thinking that the noise of splitting it would disturb my neighbours. But that morning, when I raised the chopper above my shoulders, and struck it, the result frightened me – for that large chunk of knotty wood made no more resistance than a turnip. The strength in my arm seemed to be superhuman – and I was waiting for my enemies too! Perhaps it is well for all of us that they left in the way they did. I only mention this case to show that I have enough courage, when I am certain of my enemies. But, unfortunately, a man's enemies mostly pose as his friends, and it is often hard to know one from the other.

Let me mention, in dealing with my own personal looks, how much my face has inspired others with trust and confidence. In walking the streets of London, so many strangers stop me to ask questions, that I often ask myself – 'Do they take me for a professional guide?' And when I mention that a number of these strangers are young girls just come up from the country, it can be said – 'How fortunate it is that a criminal mind is not at work behind that open face.'

But my face has passed a severer test than any of those – it is when I meet beggars, who never let me pass by without making an appeal for charity. This is the best thing to say in my favour, for beggars are, without doubt – if we make an exception of gipsies – the best judges in the world of a human face. However, I set no price myself on having this honest-looking face; for when I am out walking in search of green trees, I would rather not have my thoughts disturbed by strangers, with their minds set on things of stone, such as St Paul's and Westminster Abbey.

Again, having this open and honest-looking face is not altogether to my credit, after all; for some of our greatest criminals must have had this same face, otherwise they would have been less successful in pursuing their evil ways. I am reminded now of a little fat man with a round, smiling face, like a cherub's, whom I have often seen at street corners, watching the coming and going of certain people into certain houses. Who would have suspected that commonly dressed, lethargic little lump of being connected with a most athletic detective, to whom his information would be of great value? We would sooner connect him with some raspberry-faced old loafer, who would rather pay for that man's drinks than drink alone in selfishness.

After my ill-success with the two women I have mentioned – my blood-relation and the other – I made up my mind to trouble no more about respectable women, but to find a wife in the common streets. In fact, I could not see how I could do otherwise; for most marriages come from meeting at church or chapel, or a social gathering of some kind or other. But as I did not go to any of these places, I stood very little chance in that way. It is true that I occasionally went to a gathering of artists or literary people: but the women I met there were mostly married already; and when they were not, they bored me with their long, lifeless talk on books and art. It must be remembered that although I am now a well-known author, I was not brought up among bookmen or lovers of art. When I first met a literary man, I was over thirty years of age, so that it cannot be said that I was born to the life of literary people. Indeed, I seemed so far away from it that it appeared much more natural for me to seek a wife among the kind of people I knew before I was thirty years of age than the ones I knew later.

I will now come to my first experience – in which I tried to keep a woman long enough as my mistress to make her my wife at last. But this was no easy matter, as the next two or three chapters will prove.

CHAPTER I

Bella

IT WAS NOW THE time of the Great War, and the sexual relationship between a man and a woman had undergone a change. Prostitutes, who in times of peace would not look or speak to a common soldier, because of his small pay, were now the first to give him some attention. It was not love of country that made them do this, but safety in plying their trade. The only law in the country was a military law, and a soldier could do what he liked. It was not unusual to see a drunken soldier catch hold of a girl who was a mere child, and kiss her and frighten her too. But it was all for the country's good; half a dozen English maidenheads would be a cheap price to pay for one dead German. Very few women would have anything to do with a civilian, unless they knew him personally. The soldiers had to be served first, and I was not a soldier, for more reasons than one. Let me say here that I did not hide myself or shirk the war in any way. It will be seen from this that I did not choose a very good time in trying to find a mistress, especially in the common streets.

Under these war conditions nothing could have surprised me more than to be greeted by a woman's voice, and without giving her one look of encouragement. At that time I was passing Charing Cross, at a late hour, and the woman I have mentioned was standing in front of King Charles's statue. For the moment I thought she must be too old or too unattractive to deceive even the most drunken soldier; and that was why she, knowing a civilian's difficulty in getting a woman, thought to have more success with me. But when I looked more closely, I saw, to my surprise, that she was a fine buxom creature of about twenty-six, and the healthy colour of her face was certainly from the country.

'What are you doing here at this hour of the night?' I asked. 'You are not waiting for anyone, are you – or you would have not spoken to me.'

'No,' she answered, at once. 'I am all alone now. I have just seen my husband off to the war, five minutes ago.'

'And what are you going to do now?' I asked.

'I don't know exactly,' she answered. 'Have you any place you can take me to?'

'Certainly,' I said. 'Come along.'

As we walked on we passed several soldiers, who were looking for women; and they did not like to see a civilian walking away with so fine a prize. However, nothing happened to make either one of us feel uncomfortable. But I was very glad to leave the open street, and enter my own doorway.

This girl, whose name was Bella, did not appear to be much troubled at her husband going to the war; so I judged that there was not much love between them, which I was soon to know was the truth. I was curious to ask her a number of questions, but preferred information of her own accord. For instance, it seemed strange to me that he had left her penniless in the streets, while his own body's comfort was safe in the hands of a generous country. She was none too well dressed either, which seemed to prove that he not only held the purse, but held it too well for her liking.

From what I could gather in conversation, her story was this. That both she and her husband had come up from the country a week ago, before he left for the war. He had taken a small, cheaply furnished room for her, in a common street, and paid enough in advance to give her shelter until he could send her more money. After doing this, they both went drinking and spending money until they parted at Charing Cross Station, when they did not have sixpence between them.

'What did your husband think you were going to do for food ?' I asked.

'That was all right,' she said, 'it was understood between us that I would do a little work until he could send me some money.'

To me all this seemed to be very strange, especially as her husband's rank was above a common soldier. The man's conduct did not show much love for his wife. And the way she settled down at my place, and made herself at home, without once wondering how her husband was faring on his journey, which would perhaps be his last; whether he would return alive or fall a victim to the enemy; without appearing to even think of him at all – these things did not show much love on her part either.

If he had only known that, in less than two months, he would die in her arms; in less than two months she would go straight from his dead body to a former lover; and, meeting him at the door, would cry – 'My husband is dead now. He died fifteen minutes ago at the hospital, and I have just left his dead body. Let me come in for the night; I shall ask for no payment, for I am provided for, as the widow of a Sergeant Major.'

But, not to be before our time, we will say no more of that, and let the story take a straight course.

On the following morning, I had a long serious talk with Bella, for she had already proposed seeing more of me in the future. She could see from my surroundings that I was not a rich man, but seemed quite willing to trust me to do all I could for her. She was very pleased when I suggested that she should come to me twice a week, on Tuesdays and Fridays, and spend those days at my place; where she would cook our meals and take away what money I could afford to pay her. It was understood that she would sleep at her own lodgings, for which the rent was already paid. But if she needed anything, it did not matter about it being a Tuesday or a Friday – she could come at any time and let me know what troubled her. These matters were all arranged on a Wednesday, and I would see Bella again on Friday morning.

When this new mistress of mine had gone, I began to think

matters over seriously. For instance, if I took a strong liking to her, and the feeling was mutual, how could I keep her from her husband on his return, when the war was over? And yet, if he had not acted towards her as a good man, he could not deserve more, not even if he served his country as a fine soldier. However, these thoughts need not have worried me very much, for Bella, it seems, was fond of drink, and to me a woman that drank was not to be trusted. She confessed, on our first night, that she had been drinking all day with her husband; and one of the first questions she asked when we reached my home was whether I had any drink in the house – which I had not. When she heard this she seemed disappointed, and then said, looking at a small clock on the mantelpiece – 'I like that clock.' And when she said her first words the next morning, 'I like that clock', I came to the conclusion that all I would have to do if I wanted to get rid of Bella, without having a painful scene, would be to give her a few drinks, and then leave the house for a while. When I came back it would be certain that two faces would be missing – for there would be no Bella and no clock.

My acquaintance with Bella had now gone on for a little over a month and, with the exception of her liking for strong drink, there was not much to complain of. I don't know whether she drank a large quantity in a short time or whether a very little amount of drink affected her. Whichever it was, I was often surprised to see her in a muddled state, when she returned from doing half an hour's shopping, and I often thought that if Bella had more money to spend, she would have gone on drinking, and not have come back at all.

But there was one serious charge I had to make against her, that although I gave her the best price to pay in he market, it was quite certain that she did not return with the best things. However, I was an easygoing fellow, and only once did I offer any complaint. On that occasion I was trying to get some lather from a piece of soap that was as hard as a stone, and said – 'Bella, why don't you buy soap that I can use?'

'There is nothing at all the matter with the soap,' answered Bella, in a calm voice – 'it is the way you use it!'

When I heard this I began to wonder if there was a great art in using soap, which I, after fifty years, had not learnt; although children that were not much more than babies could master it at the first attempt.

CHAPTER II

The Trick

ONE FRIDAY MORNING, WHEN Bella came at her usual time, she began at once to tell me some great news which I knew would have some bearing on our future life. 'My husband,' she began, in a calm collected voice, 'my husband is in a very bad state of health, and is being invalided home. For that reason I shall not be able to come next Tuesday, but I hope to see you before Friday, if only for a minute or two.'

'Do what you think best,' I answered, 'but do not let your husband have the least suspicion that you have been unfaithful to him in his absence.'

'As for that,' she said – 'my unfaithfulness was more his fault than mine. But he may be worth more to me as a dead man than he was when alive, for I am thinking now of a war pension as his widow.'

On this occasion Bella was a very busy woman. She made up a large parcel to take away with her, which consisted of sheets, blankets and other articles to be washed. When I saw her working so hard, I went out for a few minutes, and returned with a bottle of whisky. I had two reasons for doing this: one was to give Bella a drink and the other was because I was expecting a friend to call that night, and I knew that he was fond of the bottle.

Bella was now ready to leave, but I asked her to wait a minute or two while I went out to get a newspaper. After that I gave her as much money as I could afford and also an extra pound which she borrowed. She then left, carrying the large, heavy parcel with the greatest ease.

Bella was a very strong girl, and I have often seen her lift a heavy armchair without straining herself in the least saying at the same time – 'Samson!' When she did this, I suggested that she should have been a nurse at the hospital, and she told me that she had once applied for such a position, and would have got it too, if she only had five pounds for the special clothes that would be needed to start her work.

When Bella had gone, I began to think how easy it was to get a mistress, and how hard it was to get a wife. Why was it so easy to get hold of other men's wives and not get one of my own? Although I did not think that Bella had now gone out of my life for ever, yet, for all that I began to think that our connection would not last much longer, and I would soon have to look for another mistress.

That night, when my friend came, I proposed a drink of whisky, which he lost no time in accepting. Taking a glass in my hand, I half-filled it with pure whisky, to show that I did not lack generosity.

'You had better fill the glass with water now,' said my friend, 'or the drink will be strong enough to skin my throat.'

'No,' I answered, adding a very little water, 'try that first.'

Raising the glass to his lips, my friend took one or two sips, and then replaced the glass on the table, saying in a voice that sounded extremely cold – 'It's all right, thank you!'

'Is it too strong or do you want some water?' I asked.

'It's all right, it's all right,' he answered, in the same lifeless voice.

I did not know what to make of this, for my friend was usually a very enthusiastic man, and, instead of my whisky giving him more ecstasy, it had robbed him of it altogether. However, I said nothing more at the time, but poured out the same quantity for myself, and added the same small amount of water. Raising the glass, I took a sip, and then another sip, and then – bang went the glass on the table. It was all water, and nothing but water; and I could have almost burst into tears. The only taste of whisky that could be detected was something like the taste of a slice of bread when it has been pointed at by a hand that has been peeling a strong onion. We looked at each other, he waiting for some explanation, and I not knowing how to make one.

At last the whole thing was clear – Bella had gone away without any intention of coming back. With this idea in her head, she had made up a large parcel, borrowed money and taken my whisky. She must have poured the whisky into another bottle, and put water in its place, during the time I had gone out for a newspaper and then added it to her parcel.

When all this became clear enough, I explained it to my friend, who at once became a different man. He shook me by the hand, with his old enthusiasm, and said – 'I congratulate you on getting rid of such a false creature although it has been done at a price.'

'Come along' I said, – 'we can still have our drink of whisky, for the "Red Lion" is only a few doors down the street.'

When I was alone that night and considered matters, I was not altogether disappointed at the result. Bella was a dangerous woman that was certain, and I was lucky in getting off so easy. It was not long before a sense of humour triumphed over it all. But I was quite mistaken in thinking that Bella had gone for ever. A woman who can tell a middle-aged man that he does not know how use soap is not without plenty of assurance.

It was not long before I had another mistress, but the conditions were slightly different. Like Bella, she did not sleep on the premises; but, unlike Bella, she came every morning and stayed till after lunch; whereas Bella, as I have said before, came for two full days every week. But we will leave this new mistress out of the question for a time, and give place to Bella's last and extraordinary visit. But even after what happened then, I could not be sure that she would not come again.

One evening, when I had an appointment with a friend, a knock came to the door just as I was ready to go. 'What a nuisance!' thought I – 'it may be an old friend, and I have no time to spare.'

But when I opened the door, I saw, to my surprise, that it was Bella, standing there with her bold face, and smiling to see me. Before I could say one word, she walked straight into the passage and began to lead the way upstairs. As soon as she was in the room, she put her arm around my neck and kissed me.

'No more of that, Bella,' I said, as soon as I had recovered from my astonishment.

'You are annoyed because I have not been to see you before,' she said – 'but it's all right now. My husband has just died in my arms, in the hospital. I'll stay here tonight with you – but don't think I want any money. By the way, I have not brought back the parcel of clothes, but will bring them tomorrow – if someone has not stolen them from my lodgings, for there are not many honest people in my neighbourhood.'

With these words, she began to undress, looking well pleased with herself, in spite of having just left a dead husband.

'Bella,' I said. 'I am very sorry for all this, and don't think any more of my clothes. To tell you the truth, I have another mistress now, but you must remember that I waited for you for a long time.'

When Bella heard this, her face became hard, for she knew now that everything was over between us. So, when I mentioned having an appointment, she prepared to accompany me downstairs. While she was putting on her hat and coat, I went into a back room to close a window, in case it should be entered during my absence. When I came back, Bella was at the head of the stairs, waiting to descend, looking a fine wench indeed, with her large leather handbag hanging on her strong naked arm. I was rather surprised that Bella, when we reached the front door, parted from me without having much to say.

It was late at night, when I returned from my appointment. As soon as I reached my room, I began to think of Bella, and considered myself lucky that she had not called in the morning, when the door would have been answered by my new mistress. I felt certain that Bella, in spite of her dishonesty, would have had her own way.

It was now bedtime, and I looked at the mantelpiece – but the clock, my pretty little clock, had gone! I was now reminded of my first meeting with Bella, and her first words almost when she had entered my room – 'I like that clock.'

After two or three minutes' thought, I felt glad that Bella had taken the clock at last, for it made me feel more certain that I would not see her again.

CHAPTER III

The Gentle Louise

I WILL NOW COME TO Louise, who had already with me for several weeks. She was a different woman altogether from Bella, and I never had cause to once doubt her honesty. She certainly enjoyed a glass of wine, but I have never known her to help herself. Unless the wine was poured out by my own hand, she would not touch it. In fact, I felt so confident in her honesty that I had duplicate keys made, so she could have the run of the house, whether I was there or not. She was a French woman, and although she did not believe in the marriage ceremony, she still believed that a man was well worth living with. She was living with another man, at the present time, but she was looking for a chance to change her lovers, if she could find one to her liking. After she had been coming to me for a little over a week, she began to take possession of the place, to my alarm. First she brought a pair of slippers, and left them there. Then came an umbrella, which she did not take away. Other things came, one by one, and remained. It was quite obvious what the result would be. For as soon as she had gathered together under my roof the things she valued and prized the most, she would quarrel with her old lover and come to the new one. She could leave him emptyhanded, for all her property would have gone before her. She did not think it worthwhile telling me what she intended to do, as she knew that I was not the kind of man to refuse her admittance if she had no home. She also knew that I liked her, and that was everything. But it was not to be, as will be seen later.

After Bella had gone, the night before, and stolen my dock, I began to wonder what kind of story I would tell Louise, when she came the next morning. As she was of a jealous disposition, I did not think it advisable to tell her the truth. My rooms were always full of little traps, which she used to examine the next morning, to see if I had had any visitors in her absence, and whether they were men or women. If I ever had lady visitors, I never let it be known to Louise, not even if they came with their own lovers or husbands. I remember how, one afternoon, a lady came to tea, with her husband. When they were leaving; the lady searched for her gloves but could not find them. The whole room was searched, also the stairs and the passage, but all in vain. So we came to the conclusion that she had dropped them in the street, before she had entered my house. But when Louise came, the following morning, she went straight to the couch, as by instinct, and, removing the pillow, brought forth a pair of lady's gloves. The lady, it seems, had placed them on the pillow and, in her restlessness, while she talked, smoked and drank tea, they had worked themselves down underneath. Louise's jealousy, on this occasion, did not last long, for she soon found a little pipe tobacco on the carpet, which was a different brand from mine, and which proved that a male visitor had been there too. But I was very much surprised when she said – 'Take care of yourself: the gloves were put there on purpose, so that if you laid your head on that pillow, you would dream of Her!'

When Louise came the next morning, it was not long, in making a quick examination of my rooms, before she missed the clock.

'Where is the beautiful little clock?' she asked, almost immediately.

'It has stopped,' I said, 'and I have taken it to a jeweller's shop to have it examined.'

This excuse would do, I thought, for a day or two; and then I would buy a new clock, saying that the jeweller had told me the other was worn out, and not worth taking away.

Louise made no answer to this, so I bent my head over a bowl of water and began to wash my face. All at once I *thought* I heard a loud scream. When I say 'thought', it must be remembered that my ears were full of little soap bubbles that were screaming like young birds, and I was not a fit judge of any other sounds that might be around me.

However, it was soon certain that I had made no mistake, for I soon had cause to turn around and ask myself – 'What has happened to the gentle Louise?'

'What have I found, you scoundrel!' she began, in a furious voice. 'You traitor with the double face: look, this shows that your heart is as treacherous as your breast – is it not? Hear me, you wicked monster: whatever agreement was made between us is castrated at once; this moment, and immediately. Look, look, you villain, and tell me what is this!'

These strange words will need some explanation. I have already said that Louise was French and, although her accent and pronunciation of English were almost perfect, yet, for all that, she often went wrong in placing her words, and did not always know their exact meaning.

What she meant by 'castrated' was 'cancelled'. And although treacherous and deceptive sometimes have the same meaning, in this case it was otherwise. For instance, one day Louise brought a very fine coat, which a tailor had left on his hands, and would sell cheaply. As she thought it would fit me, she brought it along. But when I tried it on, the size of my breast would not allow it to be buttoned; which made Louise say – 'Ah yes, you are very treacherous around the breast'; meaning of course, that my breast being bigger than it looked, was deceptive. This misuse of words was in keeping with the views of her French father, who had called Louise 'the best cow in his stable'; not knowing that to call a woman a cow would, according to English people, be a serious matter indeed.

When I heard Louise utter the above words, I was taken by surprise, and looked at her for an explanation. As soon as we were face to face, I looked at her outstretched hand, and what did I see? Two hairpins.

'Where did you find them?' I asked, not knowing what else to say.

'On the mantelpiece, where the beautiful little clock stood,' she cried with anger. 'You have given that clock to another woman, have you not?'

When I heard this, I must admit that my sense of humour, which had always served me in my dealings with Bella, could no longer help me to regard her with a little charity. The theft of clothes, the borrowed money, the whisky trick and the stolen clock – none of these things had upset me much. But to leave two hairpins in place of the clock, to cause mischief between me and my new mistress – this, I thought, was the unkindest blow of all. And how subtle it was too!

In the end I told Louise exactly what happened, and it was not long before she was convulsed with laughter. 'Poor fool!' she said at last, placing her hand affectionately on my shoulder – 'Poor fool, it is fate that everyone should take advantage of you. You are born to it. No matter, I love you all the same.'

It was strange to hear Louise using these words, for not long before that, another – a man this time – had said exactly the same thing. He was taking away some of my books to be sold, and he was to receive half share of the profits for his trouble. When he had disposed of a hundred at a ridiculously low price, he came back for the last lot, about twenty selected books in all, which I knew to be of some value. But while he was away with the last lot but one, a lady friend had paid me a visit; who, seeing what I was doing, pointed to two of the books and begged them for herself,

Now, when my friend returned and found those two books missing, he began to gasp like a fish out of water, and his lips were as white as gills. 'Two books are missing,' he said at last – 'what has become of them?'

'I have given them to a lady friend,' I answered, not understanding his strange mood. 'You have already sold more than a hundred books for a pound,' I continued – 'and I would rather give my books to a friend for nothing than sell them at so low a price.'

He said nothing to this, until he was ready to go, and the last lot of books were under his arm. It was then that he used almost the same words as Louise, saying in a voice of despair – 'Well, well, no matter; you are born to be taken advantage of, and it can't be helped.'

With these words he left the room, and it was a long time before I saw him again. On the one or two occasions that we have met since then, I have noticed that he is very careful to avoid the subject of books. I believe the last lot of books he took away was worth a number of pounds. Several people have said that one of them, in particular, was worth its weight in gold.

I don't remember Bella ever once showing any curiosity as to what kind of visitors came in her absence, and their sex; and she never once asked me how I spent time when she was not there. But Louise, flattering me with more concern, often pleased me by her little starts of jealousy. It was very laughable, one day, when a friend asked a lady to deliver a message to me, as she was passing my house, and how I saw her at the door, for one minute only. And how Louise, after a quarter of an hour's silence, shook her little fist in my face and cried sharply – 'Who would you rather have, that fat woman or me?'

Louise was a woman of thirty, but only looked her age when she was in a very serious mood, which was not often the case. At other times her face had a bright smile, which made her look no more than a young girl of sixteen. It was one of those smiles that a woman sometimes retains all through her life; that is not affected by either wrinkles, false teeth or shrunken flesh. I had once seen a fine example of this, when I met a charming woman of seventy years of age. The first thing I noticed in her was her wonderful smile, and it is the only thing I can remember, too. She had shown me a drawing of herself, done by a great master, when she was seventeen, and when I looked I saw, to my astonishment, that the portrait was as much like the woman of seventy as it was of the girl of seventeen. It was the smile that mattered, and age was out of the question.

Louise had now been with me a little over a year, and then the end came suddenly. She was taken ill, and in bed for three months. During that time I waited patiently for her, without a thought of other women. But when she was able to walk and came to see me, it was only to say that she was not coming back, and that all must now be over between us. The man she was living with had been so good to her that she had no intention of being false to him again. 'Although there is no great love on his part or mine,' she said – 'we like each other well enough to make things pleasant.'

When I heard this, I said nothing, for I knew it would all be for the best in the end. But Louise broke down and cried, when we parted at last. As for me, I went back upstairs and, lying on the bed, was in half a stupor for several hours. But when Louise did not come the next morning, after breakfast, it was then that I suffered most; especially when so many little things came under my notice, to remind me of her care, which I would no longer have.

'If I ever leave you,' she had said once – 'you will say, "What a good friend was Louise!" and be sorry you have lost me.'

Have these words come true, and do I think of Louise now? While I write these words, I am a married man, and happy; but we will leave that matter alone for the present – my brain must not work faster than my hand. But there is one thing in my house, which comes under my eyes every day; and I have only to look at it and I must think of Louise. It is a bronze bust of myself, done by a good sculptor, and full of life. The life in the lips is almost uncanny, and full of fascination. But when strangers or friends come to my house and praise the life-like quality of that bronze mould, a great lump rises in my throat, which is not caused by pride in possessing so fine a work of art, or its commercial value. One time, when I went wandering away from home, I had left Louise in charge, to come every day, in my absence, to see that everything was all right, and to keep the place clean. I was away for over a month and, when I returned, there was a welcome glow in her eyes; and everything seemed to be in its proper place, as clean and bright as her own self. But the next day, when I happened to look at my bronze head, I saw, to my surprise, that although the lips were dark and clean, yet, for all that, the nose, the eyebrows and the hair were white with dust. I could not account for this, seeing that the lips, which were so clean, protruded in the same way as the nose and the eyebrows, and were just as likely to catch the dust. However, although I thought the matter was strange, I did not think it was of sufficient interest to brood over, and dismissed the subject at once. But about three or four days after this, when Louise was in a happy mood, she pointed to my bronze head, and said in a shy, low voice – 'I came here every morning, when you were away, and never failed once: and the very first thing I did, when I entered the room, was to kiss that mouth!' So, every time I look at my bronze head, I think of the time when that hard mouth was kept clean by living lips.

Louise has gone, and it is hardly likely that I shall ever see her again; but this truth remains with me to the end of my days. She was the first woman that ever had any real affection for me; that cared for me for myself, and not for what she could get out of me, in the way of money, trinkets or clothes. She has gone, but I only have to look at that sculptured mouth, or hear a friend praise its life-like force – and a lump rises in my throat. Two women are in the room: my wife is there in the flesh; the other is there in the spirit – and that is the gentle Louise.

CHAPTER IV

The Silk Stocking

WHEN LOUISE HAD GONE, it was a long time before I could think seriously of taking another mistress. But I found it very difficult to settle down to my work, and went into society more, as much as I disliked doing so. I dislike society, because conversation exhausts my brain more than silent thought – again, I cannot hold my water long enough for a prolonged conversation; nor can I sit in comfort through a political speech or a sermon. People did not seem to dislike me, but my silence must have often bored them. If it were not for having something of a name in the world, I don't believe anyone would have given me a second invitation to their house. What was the use, as far as society goes, of knowing good music from bad, if I could not give some reason? And, although I could tell a good picture when I saw one, yet, for all that, I could not praise it like an art critic. But that I recognised a good picture, when it came under my notice, has been proved more than once. One day, when I looked into a shop window, I saw a picture of still-life – some apples on a small table. 'If I had that picture,' thought I, 'I would never be without apples – my favourite fruit – and I would have no need to worry about money, season or crop.' Looking at those apples a little longer, I was so taken with the richness of their painting that I was prepared to give half my fortune to have them in my room. Which meant that I would give ten pounds, my fortune at that time being twenty pounds. But I did not go into the shop, for two reasons. First, I thought the picture would be too much for my purse; and I did not like the idea of raising the shopkeeper's hopes that I was going to buy it and then coming out of his shop without spending a penny. The second reason was this: I always like to spend my money as though I am worth plenty more, and did not want the shopkeeper to think that I was too poor to pay the price he asked for his picture. The picture was by F——. Now as I had never heard of such an artist – although I know now that he was one of the greatest masters of that kind of work – it must be seen from this that I know a good work of art when I see one.

It was now that I met a certain strange woman, whom I would have cause to remember for a long time. One night I had gone out to have dinner with a friend, at his own house in the West End. Other friends came in for coffee after dinner, and then we all began to drink brandy. This went on for some time, and it was long after midnight when I parted with him at the door, and began walking towards my own home, which was about a mile away. With the exception of two or three policemen, standing quietly in doorways, there was no sign of human life anywhere; and the sound of my own feet on the hard pavement was an annoyance to my nerves. Under these circumstances, the reader will judge of my surprise when I say that a woman suddenly stood at my side, coming from I know not where. And when I saw, at a first glance, that she was well-dressed and ladylike in appearance, I was more surprised than ever. 'Surely,' thought I, 'this woman is not homeless; and her presence here, at two o'clock in the morning, can be no other than an accident.'

'Where are you going?' I asked, not knowing what else I could say.

'I am coming home with you,' she answered, taking hold of my arm.

'No, no,' I said hastily. 'You have made a great mistake. If you do not look for richer customers, you will soon be in rags – and my home is only the home of a poor man.'

'Come along,' she exclaimed, with a light laugh – 'I have not asked you for money. When I do, we can discuss the matter then.'

As we walked along, she began to explain matters, and I did not see any reason to think her story improbable. She told me that she had been drinking heavily, and that she had finished by drinking six strong liquors within an hour of closing time. Then, being in a high state of intoxication, she had walked the streets, not caring to return to the hotel where she was staying. And although she was now in a fit state to do so, it was too strange an hour, and she preferred to wait until the rest of the world was well awake.

'I am living apart from my husband,' she said, at last; 'but he is rich and makes me a generous allowance. For that reason, I have no need to go home with you or any other man, to make a living.'

Not long after this we reached my home, which was in a mean little street – although a stone could almost be thrown into one of the most fashionable quarters of the world. And when I opened the front door, and we both clattered up the narrow, awkward stairs that did not have one straight step, I made my companion some apology. But she only laughed, and said – 'How interesting.'

When we were in the room and seated, I asked my companion if she would have a glass of wine, which was the greatest mistake I could have made. To make matters worse, the bottle was almost empty, and I had to open another. I could not fail to see the eagerness in her face, and I knew at once that I ought not to have opened a full bottle of wine, especially at that hour. Before I had half finished my drink, hers had gone, and yet I could only remember seeing her slowly taking one or two sips, like a bird at a fountain, But when I was slow in refilling her glass, it did not take her long to remind me that it was empty, and that she would like more. So, when I saw it was a case of finishing the whole bottle, I was determined that we should not sit too long over empty glasses. When we came to the last two glasses, she said, half stupidly – 'Open another bottle.'

'This bottle was the last,' I answered – 'and we were very lucky to have it.'

'What's in that bottle on the shelf?' she asked, pointing to a far corner.

'Vinegar,' I answered.

'Bring it here and let me see,' she said.

By this time, I began to see that there was going to be trouble. However, I brought her the bottle and she was not satisfied until she had not only smelt it but tasted it too.

But I will now go back to our earlier conversation over the wine, which was so interesting to me that I began to wonder if I had found a kindred spirit, and the proper companion for a literary man. For it was not long before she had told me that her husband was the brother of a well-known author, and mentioned his name, with other well-known authors she had known. It was now that I told her that I was something of an author myself, but not with a very big name.

'Do you know the work of ——?' she asked, mentioning an author with a world-wide reputation, who had died a few years ago. 'He', she continued, 'was a great friend of my husband's and I have often had tea with him at Thirty —— street.'

I have known a number of strange coincidences in my time, but this was the strangest of all. For I had had dinner in that very house a few hours before I had met her. And when I studied the whole case from beginning to end, I did not know what to make of it. For instance, why did she mention that very house, with the thousands and thousands of other houses in London? And why should we two, both connected with literature, be brought together at that strange hour, and the only two human beings in the streets and awake? But my first thoughts that, getting a divorce from her husband, she would then marry me and put an end to mistresses and strange women, was to have a severe check, and soon too. For when she saw no sign of more wine, her mood changed suddenly, and she became hard and quarrelsome. Her voice was raised to a higher pitch, and I began to think of my neighbours who were now asleep.

At last my patience gave way altogether, and I told her in a cold quiet voice that if she did not want to settle down quietly until daylight, she could go: and that she was not only welcome to the wine, but also to the money I had given her. For I had already given her a certain sum, which she had not asked for, and which she took with the utmost indifference, and threw, in a crumpled state, into her bag.

'Do you want to go?' I asked, leading the way towards the door and expecting her to follow me.

But the only answer she made to this was to take off one of her shoes, and then the other.

The next moment she began to take off her stockings, which were of fine silk. While she was doing this, in silence, she was looking at me all the time, and I thought I saw a strange, mad light in her eyes. Her face was smiling, but I felt certain that her joy came from some wicked thought, which was soon proved to be correct. For she suddenly threw one of the stockings into my hand, and cried, in a sharp voice – 'Are you going to murder me with that?'

'Nonsense, what nonsense!' I said gently – 'What brought such a foolish idea into your mind?'

Without making a direct answer to this, she began to swish the other stocking around her own neck, saying, at the same time – 'Now is the time; the work is already half done.'

It was now that I began to feel really angry, for it was four o'clock in the morning and I needed sleep.

'Do as you like,' I said, 'stay or go; but I am going to sleep here, in this chair.'

With these words, I closed my eyes, folded my arms and settled down.

What happened after this I can only guess. I must have gone off to sleep immediately; and she, no longer having anyone to talk to, probably did the same. As I did not hear her make the least movement, she must have been very quiet; or was I myself in such an exhausted state that I could sleep through thunder?

All I know is this – I opened my eyes, in changing my position, just long enough to see two things, that it was five o'clock and that my strange companion was lying curled, almost in full dress, on top of the bed, as though she had been too sleepy to undress. 'Thank God I will soon have a sober woman to deal with,' was the quick thought that went through my brain before I fell asleep for the second time.

When it was eight o'clock, I was determined to sleep no more until I had got rid of my companion, although I felt stupid and limp from insufficient rest. Now, although I am a rough man in some ways, that can boast of neither college nor club, yet, for all that, I have been called more than once 'one of Nature's gentlemen'. Which means, I suppose, that I am a gentle man. If the term could not have been applied to me on the present occasion, I would have regretted it to the end of my life. For when I woke my companion and offered her a cup of tea, the change in her was so great that she appeared to be a different woman altogether. Her gentle voice, with its finely balanced accent, so surprised me that I said to myself – 'Surely this is not the woman who only four hours ago used foul language and talked of murder!'

And when she began to apologise for any trouble she might have given, and hoped that I would forgive her, I, not to be outdone in gentleness, said, 'You have given no trouble at all, and I hope you have rested well.'

Soon after this she was dressed and ready to go. Although I had no desire to see her again, I certainly wished her no harm. In fact, I felt pleased to know that she was not poor, and had more money coming to her every week than I could earn by my work.

But she had scarcely shook hands and said goodbye, when she saw my morning paper, for the first time, lying unopened on the table. I had brought it upstairs from the letter box while she still slept.

'Do let me see that paper before I go,' she cried suddenly, holding her hand out eagerly.

'Certainly,' I said, feeling rather awkward at her silence, while she stood near the window, reading, for what appeared to be a long time. However, it was not long before she was in the street and going, I suppose, back to her hotel lodgings.

When she had gone, I picked up the paper and the first thing I read was of a woman that had just been found murdered, strangled with her own silk stocking. This cleared up the whole mystery. My late companion had been reading of that murder the night before, and that accounted for her strange behaviour. But as I had not seen an evening paper, I knew nothing about it.

As soon as I was left alone to think of what had happened, I said to myself – 'No wonder some of these strange women are found murdered!'

I was reminded of another woman, whom I had met some time before, and gone with her to her rooms. And I remembered how she had taken up a board in the floor and shown me two bundles of treasury notes, which must have contained something like two hundred pounds. If she had done this with some men she would have been murdered in her sleep. The circumstances were very peculiar at that time. For treasury notes had only just come out for the first time, and caused so much suspicion for a week or two that some people trembled like guilty thieves when presenting them in payment. To make matters worse, shopkeepers, not having sufficient silver in hand, were refusing to cash them. This woman who now had paper money for the first time in her life, and who was poorly dressed, was so much afraid to tender these notes in payment that I believe she would have gladly sold me the whole lot for five pounds' worth of silver. Before I left her I gave her thirty shillings in coin, in exchange for two notes, advising her, at the same time, to buy a new hat and coat, and then spend her paper money without fear of being arrested. I did not ask her where the money came from, whether it was stolen or found, but told her very seriously not to show it to strange men, if she valued her own life.

CHAPTER V

Young Emma

MY ONLY FEAR IN writing this book is that my readers will think I am something of a woman-charmer; one who is always bending over a woman's shoulder, devoted to her every whim and flattering her with soft words. This is entirely wrong, for I would much prefer the company of men to women. First of all, I am a great smoker of strong tobacco, and I like to blow my heavy smoke where I like, without consulting my friends, and for that reason I often find women a nuisance. I am also fond of strong drink, and a suspicion that women count my glasses makes me feel uncomfortable. However, I have never once, in all my life, been rude to a woman. But I am so conscious of lacking the charms that please a woman that I don't think it possible that any woman could fall in love with me at first sight. Yet, strange to say, many a woman would have trusted her future life with me, after she had known me a little time. Perhaps they have thought, on a closer study, that I have enough kindness, good humour and patience to make a good husband.

My experience with Bella, and then with Louise as mistress, had taken up twelve months of my life and I was as far off as ever in getting one woman as a life companion. And after my experience with the woman with the silk stockings, I began to see that I could easily make a bad mistake that would ruin me for ever. The whole question seemed to be this – whether a woman drank or did not. Although I was a drinking man, I was very particular about this; for I did not expect any woman to have the same willpower and control as a man when it comes to taking drugs. And if it came to having children, when a tin mother would be of more value than a silver father – what would happen if she drank and neglected her home? No, no; I could live with a slovenly woman, an extravagant woman, and with a woman with a sharp tongue; but with a woman that drank I could never live. The effect of drink on men is strangely different, it makes devils of some men and angels of others. But the effect of drink on women is to make devils of them all.

I began to wonder, at this time, whether it would not be wiser to go more into society and try to get a wife that way. But the very thought that I would get a woman who would drag me into the limelight gave me an unpleasant feeling. For I hated society, and all my thoughts were set on a quiet life in the country. Every day I was thinking of green lanes, and woods with their own heaven of bluebells; and pools where I might see a kingfisher dive, to brighten his jewels with water. Not a day passed without my having such thoughts as these.

One night, about two weeks after my adventure with the silk stockings, I went forth again on the old quest. Having this idea in my mind, I had stayed at home all day – with the exception of an hour to lunch at a restaurant – so that I might be in fit condition to tramp the streets all night, if it should be needed. For I had made up my mind to make a great effort, on this particular night, to find a young woman who was not too demoralised to be saved from the streets – if someone gave her the chance.

The war had been over for some time, and the streets were no longer full of soldiers. Women were now casting their eyes on civilians, in the same way as they did before the war, and they no longer felt uncomfortable at the side of a man who did not wear the King's uniform. If a man was well-dressed and looked prosperous, he could take his choice of glad eyes and winsome smiles, followed by friendly nods. Many a strange woman who passed him by would give him the invitation; and he could raise his hat and speak without fear of accosting a respectable woman. On this occasion I was dressed smartly in a light overcoat, which was almost new, and it was this that probably made a number of women smile and come to a very slow walk, to enable me to make the next advance. But here I must make another confession which may appear strange indeed. It is this – I am a very shy man. For instance, if one of these women did not actually come to a dead halt and speak to me first, it was not at all likely that I would have turned back and followed her, however much I might have been impressed by her beauty, and however cordial might have been her greeting. Time after time have I gone out looking for a woman, and time after time have I returned home alone, because I have not had the courage to take advantage of a woman's encouragement. This is the reason why I never made a mistake in accosting a respectable married woman, in spite of my dealings with scores of other strange women, through a number of years as a single man. As far as I can remember, every woman that I have had dealings with has come up to me boldly and told me why, before I could express any thought of my own. But what I have said before, about having an honest-looking face, has stood me well in cases of this kind; for women have, more than once, given me far more encouragement than I could have expected from them.

This shyness is sometimes so painful that I have to take two or three strong drinks before I can look at a woman, in spite of having gone out on purpose to meet one. I am very pleased to be able to make this confession; otherwise in the following adventure I would appear like the strong, crafty, designing man of middle age on the look-out for a young and innocent girl.

It was now eleven o'clock, and I was standing at the end of the Edgware Road, near the spot where the Tree of Tyburn had stood. There were quite a number of women and young girls walking to and fro, but none of them seemed to take my fancy. Some of them were the worse for drink, and I was determined to have no more to do with a woman of that kind. All at once a bus stopped right in front of me, and I looked, half wondering what kind of passengers would alight. There was only one; and that was a young girl who could be anything between fifteen and twenty years of age. Thinking of her youth, I began to turn my eyes away, but the smile on her face would not allow me to dismiss my interest in that way. Not only that, but it soon became obvious that the smile was meant for me. If I had any doubt, it was to go at once, for, in passing close by, she nodded slightly, and almost came to a halt. But although I raised my hat in acknowledgment and returned her smile, my old feeling of shyness came back to me, and I made no effort to overtake her. However, when she turned her head and saw that I was not following her, she, apparently liking my appearance too well to lose me, stood looking my way, and waiting to see what I intended to do. When I saw this, and knew that the hour was late and that the streets would soon be almost empty of human life, I mustered up enough courage to approach her and to ask her where she was going.

'I have spent the evening with some friends, and am now going home,' she said.

'Will you come to my home instead?' I asked, knowing what her answer would be, for I had only approached her after much encouragement.

'Yes,' she answered simply, without asking any questions, and with absolute trust.

With this simple word, she took hold of my arm. I believed, at that time, that she took my arm because of a little fear of older women who glanced darkly at her in passing; jealous and angry that she – a young and simple-looking little creature – had succeeded in getting a male companion and they had not. But when I knew her better, I came to the conclusion that natural affection had as much to do with it as any fear she might have had of her own jealous sex.

As we passed the Marble Arch, going towards Holborn, I cannot say that I felt comfortable. I began to wonder what people thought of seeing a well-dressed man of middle age walking side by side with a young girl that was poorly dressed. Her age was twenty-three, but with her short skirt and a soft, saucy-looking little velvet cap with tassels, she did not look a day more than fifteen. I seemed to have a fear that some inspector of morals would come up to us, and say to me – 'What's that child to you, and where are you taking her?' And I had to admit, in my own mind, that if this happened, it would be a right and proper thing to do, and a credit to the country – even though it had no sympathy with me. Thinking of this, I took my companion through the back streets, which made the distance to my home a little longer, but not much.

As we passed under the street lamps, I looked sideways at my companion, and was well satisfied with her appearance; and once or twice I stopped and lit my pipe, when we were in dark places, as an excuse to look into her eyes. But what struck me more than anything else was the softness and tenderness around her mouth. I was very pleased to see this; for it was a sure proof that my companion had had very little to do with men, and was not a professional street-walker. If she had been that, it would have been certain that her mouth would have been firm and hard, and no softer for a smile that was forced and false.

When we reached my rooms, I asked my companion if she would have a glass of wine.

'No, no,' she answered, quickly – 'I never touch strong drink in any form, but I would like a cup of tea, if it is not too much trouble to make it.'

'This is a good beginning,' I thought, thinking of Bella and the woman with the silk stockings.

Soon after this she began to tell me, in answer to my questions, something about her own life. First of all she surprised me by saying that she was in steady work, in the city; but that the place closed on Friday night and did not open again until Monday morning. For that reason she had to live with some friends during the weekends, and pay them for her board and lodging. However, she did not like the place very much, and intended to give a week's notice on Monday, when she returned; as they did not pay her sufficient wages.

When I heard this, I understood a good many things, or, at least, thought I did. This poor girl was one of a great number of others, who worked for a starved wage and was forced to occasional immorality. Such were my thoughts, but they were not altogether right, as will be seen later on.

It was not long before I made up my mind to try and win this young girl's love, with the object of marriage. I flattered myself that she had already taken a liking to me. As she did not have to go back to work the next morning, I promised myself a long conversation with her, in which I would make her certain offers. What that conversation was about, and its result, will be told in the following chapters.

CHAPTER VI

The Complaint

THE NEXT DAY WAS Saturday, and young Emma, my new mistress, was away from work for the weekend.

'What will your friends say, when you go to them this morning, to know that you were away all night?' I asked. 'Will they suspect you of leading a fast and a double life?'

'Not at all,' she answered, 'I will say that I have stayed with my other friends, whom I had just left before I met you. And as my friends do not know each other, the truth can never be known.'

On further conversation I found that she was a country girl, and had no relatives in London; and the only friends she had were the people she had visited the night before, and the people she should have gone to after, instead of going home with a strange man.

During the night I had lain awake for a long time, and made my plans. But now, when the time came for speaking them, I began to doubt their wisdom. It did not seem to me a right thing that I, a man who was old enough to be her father, should try to bind her young life to mine. And yet it was quite obvious to me that she could do much worse; that she would take to a fast life and die young. In that case I, though twice her age, might very well survive her by a quarter of a century. However, there was no time to be wasted, for she would be leaving me soon, and I did not want it to be for ever. So I began in this way – 'You are giving your employer a week's notice on Monday, but you do not appear to have any prospect of another place. Now, if you care to come here and look after my comfort, you will be certain to find a kind and an easy master.'

'Very well,' she answered, with a soft laugh – 'we'll try our luck together. You can expect me here in a week's time, on Saturday morning, about ten o'clock. Will that do?'

It did not surprise me in the least to hear her say this; for, after all, she would always be free to leave me at a moment's notice, if she was not satisfied with my treatment. And as I would have to trust her with money for housekeeping, there would be no need for her to go away without a penny in her pocket.

In case she should alter her mind, thinking, from my present squalid surroundings, that I would be too poor for any luxury that was not a dream, I gave her a little more account of myself, and what she could expect.

'I am not so poor that I cannot live in a better place than this,' I said, 'but in these days it is very difficult to make a change, owing to the shortage of houses. But as soon as we are able to move,' I continued, 'we will; and we will buy more furniture, and take a pride in making a better home.'

Not long after this I wished her goodbye, and she left, with the promise to come back to me in a week's time. Strange to say, I had looked forward to her going, for I wanted to sit down for an hour alone, and enjoy her in the spirit and as a pleasant dream. However, it was not long before my feelings changed entirely. I soon began to ask myself – 'How can I live without her for a whole week?' And I began to think of what a fool I had been in not asking her where she worked, so that I might be able to see her. In the end I began to curse myself for letting her go at all. 'Why should she give her employer a week's notice?' I asked myself. He, with his low, starvation wages, had no consideration for her, then why should she study him? She had already told me that she kept nothing there that was worth bringing away, and that all her clothes were at her weekend lodgings. For that reason it would be quite as easy for her to leave at once as to leave empty-handed in a week's time. What annoyed me was this – if I had suggested such a thing, no doubt she would have agreed. 'If, through this stupidity, I lose her altogether,' thought I, 'I have only myself to blame.'

But these thoughts were gentle compared to the one that followed. For I suddenly had a vision of that young girl – not working quietly in a shop or warehouse – but parading the streets and attracting the notice of men. I saw her walking lightly and shaking the tassels on her velvet cap; as proud of her grace and beauty as a black horse, when he prances at a funeral. Smiling here and there, her actions seemed to cry out – 'Who'll buy, who'll buy a thing dainty and young? You there, smoking the large cigar, shall I say, "Sold again and got the money"?'

This thought became so terrible at last that I could no longer remain indoors, writing; in spite of having certain other thoughts that were eager for expression and whimpered at the long delay. 'If she's guilty of this kind of life,' thought I, 'I am sure to find it out. She will not be able to keep away from her old haunts for a whole week; and if I am there, night and day, how can she escape me? Although she may not come close, my sight is wonderful for seeing a long distance off.'

With this thought taking full possession of my mind, I left the house, and made my way towards the Marble Arch. But I walked very slowly, for my eyes began to work at once, searching in every direction, to find a young girl with a velvet cap. This velvet cap had become more important to me than my father's waistcoat, which is all I can remember of him. My father had died young, when I was very small, and I cannot remember whether his face was bearded or smooth, or whether he was lean or fat. All I can remember of him is the soft velvet waistcoat, on which I could lay my face and sleep; loving him for that warmth and comfort, while he was loving me for myself, and giving me the care of a father. He was a small man, I have been told – like myself; but he had a weak chest, and coughed like a giant.

In about half an hour I reached the Marble Arch and, passing it by, stood at the end of the Edgware Road, in the exact place where I had met young Emma. But not seeing any signs of her, it was not long before I began to reason with myself. For instance, this young girl would not have the strength to keep walking day and night; and, if she walked at night, she must rest by day. With this thought, I crossed the road and went into Hyde Park, where so many of these unfortunate streetwalkers take their daily rest.

But although I saw scores of girls and women sitting in chairs and on the free seats, I could not see one that resembled in any way the girl I was searching for. However, I decided to sit down myself, taking a position that would command a long distance through the Park, and trusting to my eyes to make no mistake. Once or twice I trembled with excitement as I caught sight of a blue cap in the distance; but it was not long before I decided that the woman was too thin or too fat, too tall or too short to be the one I searched for, and dreaded to find. However, I made up my mind to remain in that neighbourhood until midnight, and have my meals there, before I returned home. The hours seemed to go heavily and slow, no matter what I did. It was all the same, whether I sat on a seat in the Park or drank tea in one place or ale in another – the time did not pass any the more quickly. At ten o'clock I was standing at the end of the Edgware Road, but none of the buses that stopped there discharged a young girl with a velvet cap. But all at once I saw a couple of people in the distance – 'That's her,' thought I – 'I have found her at last.'

I stepped back against the wall to let them pass. In doing this I had turned my eyes away, for not more than a second, but when I looked again, the both of them had vanished. 'They are gone indoors,' thought I, walking up the street.

It was not long before I came to a public house. 'They are in here,' I said to myself. The door was wide open, and I looked in, but only saw a number of men. However, I went inside and called for a drink, so that I might be able to see into every corner of the place. Yes, there was one woman there, sitting in a corner at the side of the door; but while I looked, she was joined by a man, who had just been served with drinks and was carrying them from the bar. I could see at a glance that this woman had not the remotest resemblance to the one I sought. Her hat was not only not of velvet, but was also of an entirely different shape, and she was old enough to be young Emma's mother. 'Surely,' thought I, 'I must be going mad, to make a mistake like this.'

It was very fortunate, at this time, I was reminded of an adventure in the past, when a similar state of feelings had possessed me. On that occasion I was crossing a desert, which I had been told could be crossed in four days. So I took enough food with me to last three days, thinking a fast on the last day would do me more good than harm. But I was wrongly informed for, on the fourth day when my provisions were all gone, I could still see no sign of a house, much less a village or a town. The consequence was that when I did see a house, at last, in the far distance, I was in a bad state indeed, being light headed with hunger. My eyes were playing me such bad tricks, that I began to pounce on objects to the right and left of me, mistaking them for various forms of food.

Thinking of this adventure had a good effect on me, on the present occasion, for it brought back my common sense. I knew that if I was not careful, the same state of feeling would come again. And, even as I once mistook stones for hunks of bread, so would I now, if I did not restrain myself, see velvet caps in every direction, and tassels hanging to them all.

With my thoughts under better control, I began to make my way home, for the hour was getting late. But never once, until I was indoors for the night, did my eyes forget my morning command – to search the streets in every direction for a young girl wearing a blue velvet cap with tassels hanging to it.

I spent the next day in much the same way, and also the days that followed, until Saturday morning came at last; when I was to expect young Emma at ten o'clock. As I lived above a shop, the front door was opened early in the morning, and left open all day; and visitors could walk straight up my stairs and knock at my private door, without waiting for an answer in the open street.

The great morning came at last; the morning that was to alter the whole course of my future life. But instead of feeling proud and happy at the prospect of meeting a new love, whom I had even hope of making my bride – instead of this, I was sitting limp in a chair, and in a wretched state of unhappiness. My breath, which, owing to a feeling of sickness, made every effort to groan or sigh, came either too fast or too slow, and I was trying to get it under proper control. 'What a fool I have been,' I muttered to myself, bitterly. 'To think that I, with all my experience in life, and all my years, have learnt nothing, nothing at all.'

I looked at the clock, but cannot say why; for time did not matter now – it was quite certain that I would see no more of young Emma and her velvet cap. She would keep away in fear of her life. For when one of these girls gives a man a venereal disease, she is even afraid to meet him in the open street, where thousands would protect her from violence; and she would be foolish indeed if she did not change her haunts for a while.

'No wonder,' thought I, 'she was not to be seen anywhere near the Marble Arch; she was more likely to be found at Charing Cross or near St Paul's. It is quite certain that she will not come here and meet her victim all alone, in his own room.'

But although I had these thoughts, it must not be imagined for one moment that I would do this poor girl any harm. On the contrary, I pitied her, as much as I pitied myself at having lost her. Although I was certain that she would not dare to come again yet, for all that, I still remembered her with a strange pleasure. I was still concerned about her more than about myself.

It was not long before all my thoughts ended in sorrow for her, and I cared nothing for my own life. It did not take me long to come to the conclusion that I would soon be all right again, as far as the body was concerned. My constitution was strong, and my health had always been good. Knowing this, I had every confidence that this complaint would not do me much harm, and would only cause me a little inconvenience for a month, or perhaps a little longer. 'To a doctor,' thought I, 'this will not be much more than a laughing matter, and I already know his advice – "Don't drink, and don't worry."'

My experience with women, after all this time, had led me nowhere; for I was now as far off as ever in getting a companion for life. Bella was a thief; Louise was an invalid; the woman with the silk stockings was a drunkard; and now, young Emma ——

But I had no sooner come to this name than there was a gentle knock at the door. When I heard this, my heart leapt in my body, and for a moment I could not believe my ears.

The next moment a young girl, wearing a velvet cap, walked into the room, without waiting for the door to be opened for her, and as though the place belonged to her and she only knocked from politeness. It was young Emma, with her smiling face, and the trim tassels on her shoulder. But what amazed me most, was the innocence in her face.

CHAPTER VII

The Break Down

THAT I WAS GLAD to see young Emma again, it is needless to say; but I was determined to speak openly to her. Even after what had happened it was impossible to associate that young girl, with her candid face, with any evil intention. However, she was still so much of a child that I knew that nothing in the way of disease would shock or disgust her; and that if I used gentle language, I could tell her the worst things without fear of frightening her and driving her away. She was still so much of a child that she knew nothing wrong or improper in a love that kissed in the middle of meals. Knowing this, I began at once, as soon as I had greeted her and she had sat down.

'Since you were here, I have contracted a disease,' I said quickly – 'and I am very much afraid, Emma, that you are to blame. However, it is not very serious, I hope, and I am glad the long week is over, and you have come back to me.'

But if I had expected this news to frighten her and her to show a guilty face, I was to be mistaken. For all she did was to turn to me quickly, and say, with more seriousness than she had yet shown – 'If I had done that, do you think I would have come back to you?'

The logic of this was so plain and simple that I began to wonder why, as soon as I saw that girl's face at the door, I had not reasoned in the same way. Of course she would not have come back – unless she were mad and wanted to be strangled with her tassels, as the other woman, who had asked to be murdered with her silk stockings.

The only answer I made to her remark was to kiss her and say, 'We will let that subject drop, for the present; you are now my little housekeeper, and I hope you will be more than that before long.'

We had a lot to say to each other about the long week that had just passed. 'It was almost unbearable,' she said. 'On two or three occasions, when I had a chance, I passed through your street, but thought you would not like it if I called to see you. At one time I thought I saw you in the street and followed a strange man, and almost spoke to him before I saw my mistake.'

When I heard this, I was very pleased indeed. She, it seems, had been in something of the same state as myself when I searched for velvet caps, and thought I saw them too. But with the exception of saying that I too had found the week long and tedious, I said nothing of my greater feelings when I had stood for hours with my back to the Marble Arch. I let her talk candidly, telling the truth about her own feelings, like a little child, but said nothing about my own. That she had taken a liking to me was quite obvious; but whether that flower would ever become fruit would depend on my own warmth and light. If she was not capable of a strong passion, it would die of its own weakness, and no power of mine could help it to survive.

When we at last came to practical matters, I gave young Emma a one pound note to begin her housekeeping, telling her to let me know when she needed more money. But although she consulted my taste in the matter of food, I made no special mention of certain things, and only said – 'I like everything in the way of food, so long as it is fresh and pure.' This was said so as to make her free to consult her own taste first. This freedom gave her great pleasure, for at the place where she had worked she had been sickened by a plain, monotonous diet that had no variety, and now was her chance for other, if not better things. Not only that, but I know that the stomach played a much more important part in this young girl's life than it did in mine. To prove this, I only had to say – 'Would you like to order a chicken for the weekend ?' and then to note the effect. Her voice at once became sweeter, like a bird that is grateful after rain, and the extra light in her eyes was a thing to remember.

I was now under medical treatment, but walked to and fro to the doctor's without feeling any change for the worse in my health. My little housekeeper went out to do her shopping, but was never absent for more than ten or twenty minutes. She appeared to be very happy, and yet, sometimes, she gave me the impression of having something on her mind.

'Don't sit there smiling at me in admiration,' I said to her one day, 'but tell me this – have you ever had a lover in the past whom you sometimes think of now?'

Her only answer to this was to throw her arms around my neck, and explain – 'Dear Old Funny Cuts!' This was before she had promoted me to the more dignified name of 'Bunnykins', which was to be permanent.

In the past I had lived on a very spare amount of kisses; but at the present time, with young Emma in the house, my income must have been considerably over fifty a day. Sometimes they came suddenly, in quick little showers; and sometimes a single kiss hovered over my face like a hawk, while I lay wondering where the attack would come, to lips, cheeks, neck or forehead.

To please young Emma I did not accept many social engagements, knowing that she did not like to be left alone. One night, when I had gone out to dinner, and returned late, I could see at once that something had happened to affect her nerves. It was not long before she told me that outside a public house, only a few doors away, there had been a terrible fight, which was almost a riot. This, of course, was a bad experience for a young girl; although, as a man, I knew well that there was never much damage done in those noisy, drunken brawls; and the sum and total of all that noise was probably two blackened eyes and one bloody nose. But when I told young Emma this, she was not convinced, saying that the yells and curses and the scuffling of feet were terrible to hear.

Two or three weeks after this I accepted another engagement to dine with a friend, but told young Emma that I would be home early, before the public houses closed, for it was always after that that the disturbances occurred. This was a friend who had done me several kindnesses, which should not be forgotten.

'Emma,' I said, 'I will be back home at ten o'clock, for certain. Now, why don't you run down to Chelsea and see your friends? You will be back here before the public houses close, and I shall be with you soon after.'

This idea seemed to please her. It pleased me too, to think that she was not being left there alone; for, at that time, I was the only resident in the house after the business people, who worked on the ground floor, had locked up for the night and gone away.

Some of my friends were drinking men and, being a drinking man myself, it was a pleasure to meet them, providing it was not often enough to interfere with my creative work, which was my greatest joy in life. But at his time I was forced, by medical advice, to be a total abstainer, and it was no more pleasure for me to meet friends of that kind than it was for them to meet me. Under these circumstances, I was very glad when the dinner was over, especially as my friend did not seem to enjoy his wine without someone to share the bottle. It did not please me at all to see his indifference to good wine; and if he had enjoyed it more it would have pleased me less, as it would have shown no sympathy with a friend's misfortune.

There was also another reason why I wished to leave and get home as quickly as possible. All through the dinner I had felt a little niggling pain in my ankle, which at times took the form of sudden stabs. It was the first experience I had ever had of that kind and, being a mystery, it frightened me. 'The band is only just tuning up,' thought I, as another vicious stab went through my ankle – 'and I had better get home and to bed before it begins to play in full earnest.'

When I arrived home, I found young Emma waiting for me, as

I had expected. But I was very much surprised to hear that she had not been out for one moment during my absence.

'You did not go to your friends at Chelsea, then ?' I asked.

'No,' she answered, 'I would rather sit here and wait for you; and you are a good Bunnykins to come home so early.'

The first thing I did, on arriving home, was to examine my foot, which was so swollen that it was difficult to get the boot off. 'Surely I have not packed my two feet into one boot,' I said, to make young Emma laugh and to save her from worry. At that moment, I had every hope that a night's rest would reduce the swelling, or a night and a day at most.

All through the night I felt pain, but not enough to keep me awake. But when I saw, the next morning, what a bloated, boneless thing my foot was, I knew that I would need more than one day's rest; especially when I put that foot out of bed and tried to stand on it. Before the day was out I began to realise that I was in for a serious illness; my temperature began to rise, and I became feverish. So I sent young Emma out for another doctor, as the old one was an invalid himself, and only saw patients at his own house.

When the new doctor had come, and I had given him enough information to work on, he said, shaking his head rather hopelessly – 'You have a certain form of rheumatism, the result of blood poisoning by a venereal disease; and I am afraid it will last long enough to need great patience. But we will hope for the best.'

As soon as he had gone, young Emma ran upstairs, to know the result, which I soon told her. 'Now, Emma,' I said, with a smile and a laugh – 'now Emma, as you have half-killed me, will you be kind enough to nurse me back to life and good health?'

Seeing that I was always trying to say something humorous, to make her laugh, she took this to be a joke, and answered – 'You must have your foot bathed in boiling water, this very moment.'

My illness was much more serious than I had expected. I suffered intense pain in secret, but laughed and joked; in fear that young Emma would think I was dying, and run away. One morning I lost the use of my two arms, and the great little woman had to wash my face and comb my hair. Her tenderness and her close attention was a mystery to me, for I could not flatter myself that it was love. I began to think it was her guilty conscience that made her so tender and affectionate; and that she was determined to make some amends for what she had done. This thought was very pleasant to me, and made me think she was a good girl, after all. But in this idea of a guilty conscience I was mistaken, as will be seen.

One morning, when young Emma was carefully arranging my pillow, and was smiling happily, I said – 'You seem to be so happy that I almost dread the return of my health.'

'I am happy because I am doing the work I am used to,' she answered – 'for I have done these things so often at home, beginning when I was a little child at school.'

It was now, for the first time, that young Emma began to tell me something about her own home and family, which I listened to with close attention. Her father, it seems, had been an invalid for a number of years before his death, and sometimes had to take to his bed for a month, and sometimes more, so that his wife often had to sit up all night and attend to his wants. This meant that there had to be another, to give the night watcher a chance to sleep by day. And as the family was too poor to hire a nurse or outdoor assistance, and lived on a lonely farm with no near neighbours – under these circumstances young Emma had to be called up for duty, even before her fourteenth year. Now, when her father was not in pain, though lying helpless in bed, young Emma enjoyed herself very much. For her father was a bigger and a much more wonderful doll than the little wax figure she had been accustomed to wash, dress and fondle. She washed her father's hands and face, and dried them too. She combed his hair, time after time, and made it into curls, which he seemed to enjoy as much as herself. The only time he became serious and cried out in alarm was when he saw little Emma standing near the bed with a pair of scissors in her hand, ready to cut his hair. But in spite of all her pleading, he still refused to give her permission to do that.

This had been young Emma's experience as a child, and I could now see the reason why it gave her so much joy to bathe my foot, to wash my hands, and to comb my hair. For it must be remembered that she was still no more than a child; and it never once occurred to her that I might die – no more than it had in the past when she had attended on her father.

But what interested me most in her story was that it seemed to throw a light on her own taste, and gave some explanation of her attitude towards myself. Her father had been a number of years older than her mother, and they had both led a very happy life. Then why should their daughter not fall in love with a man that was old enough to be her father, even as her mother had done before her? And although her father had been a great trouble, it must be remembered that he did not die of old age, but of a severe chill caught in the fields, while pursuing his occupation, which led to other complaints. So, though he had left his wife a long widowhood, it was due to an accident, and not to nature.

While young Emma was telling me these things, she was still combing my rebellious hair, which still refused to take any other shape than the one to which its master had trained it for many and many a year.

CHAPTER VIII

A Night of Horror

IT DID NOT TAKE me many days to know that my illness was going to be stubborn and long, in spite of rest, medical treatment, and young Emma's care. Although I no longer suffered pain, except for aching bones, caused by lying so long in bed, yet for all that, my foot was still fat and bloated, and still showed no sign of being different. Unfortunately I was suffering something worse than pain; it was a sick feeling which came over me occasionally, when my life felt sinking lower and lower, until I thought the very end had come. My courage always failed me then, and I could no longer try to make young Emma laugh. And when my great little nurse realised for the first time, that her patient was unusually quiet and asked, 'Are you sleeping, Bunnykins?' – she received no answer, for I had no courage to say, 'No' and give the reason why.

At this time I was lying on a couch in my sitting room, my bedroom being the room below. And every night young Emma brought up a mattress and bedclothes and slept on the floor at my side, so as to be near me through the night. These things she removed in the morning, in case anyone came to see me. For some reason or other, she seemed to need my company almost as much as I needed hers, and would not sleep in the room below all alone.

One night, when I woke about the middle hour, I saw. to my surprise that young Emma was sitting up straight, with her head bowed, and her two hands clasping her knees. 'Surely she is not dreaming,' thought I, 'and going to walk in her sleep, while I look on helplessly, and without power to reach her.' But just as I was about to speak to her, she unclasped her hands and began to lie down, making a few light sounds, which might have been either moans or talking in her sleep. But although I lay awake for more than two hours after this, she did not move again.

The next morning I told her what had happened in the night, and asked her if she had any knowledge of it.

'Yes,' she said, 'I sometimes have severe pains in my back, but they soon pass away. I had a bad attack of influenza during the epidemic, and since then those pains come on me occasionally. But I would not like to walk in my sleep – unless I walked to my Bunnykins.'

When I heard this, I told her to go to my doctor at once and be treated for her complaint. This she did, and returned with a box of pills and a bottle of medicine. So now we were two invalids, under the same doctor. We made a great laughing matter of our race back to health, each one determined to come in first. She claimed an advantage from youth; while I swore by a life that had been toughened by years.

Not long after this her attacks not only became more frequent, but also became more painful, and it was not long before she broke down altogether. One afternoon she had gone downstairs to prepare tea, about four o'clock. But she was so long away that I began to wonder if there was anything serious the matter. And when I heard her at last on the stairs, she was walking with so rnuch labour that I became alarmed. To make matters worse, she halted halfway, and I did not know, when she moved again, whether she would succeed in climbing the stairs or fall backward and break her neck. It was a great relief when she reached my door and entered the room. But I saw at once that there was something wrong with her; and there was no need for her to say, as she did – 'There you are, Bunnykins, you must now help yourself, for I can do no more.' The next moment she staggered to the door, and while I was lying there without the power to stand on my feet, I could hear her groping her way painfully and slowly down the stairs to the room below.

Needless to say I did not help myself, and the tea remained there, at the side of my couch, for hours, until it was removed at last by a strange woman. 'We are now at the mercy of strangers,' thought I, and wondered what would happen next.

Not long after this, I began to hear groans and cries of pain coming from the room below me. These sounds became so loud and violent at last, that I could hear the people in the street coming to a halt under young Emma's window, to listen and talk. It was not long before one or two of them, at the risk of interfering in a private matter, entered the shop, and said to the woman in charge of it – 'There is a woman here in great pain. Can nothing be done for her?'

This woman, who had not been very friendly towards us, suspecting that young Emma was more of a mistress to me than a housekeeper, became alarmed at this, and answered that she would go at once and make an enquiry.

As soon as she had seen young Emma, she came hurrying up to me and said – 'Your little housekeeper is in a terrible condition, complaining that something in her inside has fallen down, and she is suffering great pain. Shall I go for a doctor?'

But there was no doctor to be found; they were either out of town or visiting other friends. I suspect too that my address in a small, narrow alley, did not appeal to one or two of them, in their fine West End mansions – when their servants announced it. Strange to say, it did not occur to me to send for my own doctor, and hers too. However, when the woman told me of her failure, I thought of it then. But when she reached his house, she heard that he was not at home and would not be back for an hour or more. So there was nothing to do but wait.

It was almost two hours before my doctor came, and the poor girl was in agony, and crying for help all that time, while I lay upstairs listening, without any power to move. This was no fault of the doctor's, of course, for he had come at once on hearing that he was wanted at my place. But every time the poor child cried out for the doctor, it seemed to me like a cry in the wilderness, where it would be impossible to get even an echo for an answer. I expected every cry to be the last, and imagined her to be drowning and sinking for the last time, with one little hand above the water, and no one to see or take hold of it. 'To be tortured here all this time by another's agony, while in this helpless state,' thought I, 'is a cruel thing indeed.'

When the doctor arrived at last, he was only with her a few minutes, but seemed to have given her instant relief, as far as pain was concerned. But as he had to hurry away to attend another serious case, he did not come to see me, and only sent a message to say that he was to call on me professionally the following day.

It was six o'clock when the manageress came upstairs with this message. She also had something to say of her own – 'Your housekeeper must now go to the hospital,' she said, 'before she bleeds to death. The doctor has only rendered first aid, and there is more serious trouble to follow.'

With these words she left the room, with the object of getting young Emma to the hospital as soon as possible.

But at eight o'clock that night, two hours after the doctor had gone away, young Emma was still lying on the bed, and losing blood all the time. The manageress had been in communication with several hospitals, without any success. They were either full of patients or did not take in cases of that kind. When it was nine o'clock, the woman came up to me again and said – 'What are we to do? I have every fear that she will bleed to death if something is not done at once.' At last it was decided to go to the police station and see the inspector in charge, and explain the matter to him. But when the inspector had heard the whole story, he nodded his head and said – 'I am very sorry, but this is not a case for the police.'

It was now half past nine, and the woman did not know what to do. However, when she was returning she accosted a police constable, who was on duty near us, and insisted on him entering the house and seeing the girl for himself. She had no sooner done this than he came up to me at once and said – 'The girl looks dying, and something must be done. Now, if I have the police ambulance brought along, to remove her to the hospital, are you willing to pay the expenses, which will be a pound or more?'

'Certainly,' I answered, 'I will pay more than that, if it is necessary.'

'It is a very difficult case,' continued the police constable, 'because she is inside a house. When we pick up a woman in the open streets, we generally manage to get her into a hospital in twenty minutes or half an hour.'

'We have made a mistake,' I said. 'If this poor girl had been thrown into the gutter or placed on someone's doorstep, she would have been sure of hospital treatment in a very short time – is that right?'

'That's quite right, sir,' answered the police constable as he left the room.

It was now ten o'clock, and there was not a sound coming up from the room below. The silence to me appeared to be much more terrible than the sounds, when young Emma had cried in a loud voice, for someone's help. But there was nothing to be done, only to wait patiently for the ambulance. It was almost half an hour before it came, and the clock at Westminster was striking the hour of eleven when young Emma was being carried downstairs. This made it seven hours since she was taken ill, and she was not in the hospital yet.

Another unpleasant feature of the case was this: the sight of a police ambulance standing at my front door caused fifty or sixty people to assemble there; and as the public houses had only just closed, more than half the people were the worse for drink. So that when young Emma was being put in the ambulance, she was greeted by a Babel of sounds, some crying a drunken pity, others making the sound of hissing with their lips, and others uttering ribald jokes, all of which I heard as I lay helpless on my couch.

What a pity this beautiful, green world should have become verminous with humanity.

It was certainly a great relief when I heard the ambulance going off, although I had a fear that it was too late and that young Emma would not recover from the long delay. But the trouble was not over yet, it seems; for when she reached the hospital, they refused to take her in in spite of the doctor's letter saying it was an urgent case. And it was not until one of the doctors had come out to see her, and reported in her favour, that young Emma was admitted into the hospital. I am only giving the bare facts, as things happened, and make no comments.

I will now go back a little way, to the time when the ambulance was at my door. It was then that the woman who managed the shop below came up to see me for the last time, to get money from me to pay the ambulance men when it was all over.

'I don't mind speaking to you on this matter,' she said, 'because I am a mother. Your housekeeper has gone with a six months' child, which the doctor has removed. But although the child is dead, it is certainly an awkward position for you – if anything happens to the mother.'

My surprise at hearing this almost took my breath away, for I had never thought, for one moment, that young Emma was in that delicate condition, neither did the woman below, for that matter. And that that woman did not suspect anything of the kind is most surprising; for she did not like young Emma, because, I suppose, of her great youth and beauty. She would have been very glad to know that the plumpness of young Emma's body was her shame and not her pride; and that that fair body was rounded off by an unborn bastard. But the woman had no more suspicion than I had, and was as much surprised as myself when the truth became known.

When I began to weigh these words, after the woman had left my room, a good many things became clear to me, unless I was much mistaken. I have already said that I sometimes had an impression that young Emma had something on her mind; and here it was, a serious thing indeed for a young girl without any prospect of marriage.

As I sat thinking and thinking, the whole mystery seemed to unfold itself. One lighted part seemed to light another, until very little was left to provoke my curiosity. For instance, it was quite clear to me now why she intended to leave her situation. It was not because of low wages, but because she was about to become a mother. She was giving her employer notice to save herself the shame and mortification of receiving notice from him, which, if she remained there any longer, must soon happen. When I had reasoned as far as this, it also became clear why young Emma had taken to me, and so affectionately too. She had left her situation because she was about to become a mother; and she had taken to me because she was in search of a father. And now, no longer in fear of becoming a mother, and no longer in search of a father – what will she think of me, when she is fit and well, and her worst trouble is over? Will she still think that a man who is old enough to be her father is the kind of man to be her lover? The answer I made to this question was certainly not in my own favour; but I could hardly blame young Emma if she changed her feelings under the different conditions that were coming. But there was still a little hope, when I remembered how her mother had married a man much older than herself; for there is nothing stronger in the world than a mother's example. What I wanted was not her gratitude for anything I ought to have done for her, but her love, and as strong as she liked to make it. If I could not have that, there was no reason why we should ever meet again.

It was not long before I began to think of our first meeting and how strange it was. We had come together with as much ease as two drops of rain on a leaf, when the wind shakes it. One look into my face and one look into hers, and we trusted each other immediately.

'If, after all,' thought I, 'young Emma never comes back' and thinks I am not worth seeing again, even for a few minutes – if this should happen – what am I to with this foolish face of mine: why does it look so kind and honest that everyone takes advantage of it; that even this young girl from the country could see at once her chance to play her own part, without any question of what became of me in the end?' At this time I was thinking rapidly, and I soon came to the most terrible thought of all – suppose young Emma was dead: it would not have been a very serious case, I believed, if our civilised state, with its numerous doctors, hospitals and police, had moved at a reasonable pace; but a delay of nearly eight hours, when a person is losing blood all the time, is a great temptation to Death. When I came to this thought, I was none too hopeful, and feared for the worst.

It was now that I began to think of the words used by the woman below, when she had said – 'It is certainly an awkward position for you, if anything happens to the mother.'

Yes, the position would be painful indeed, and I was distracted with the thought of it. I could see her mother, a plain simple creature up for the first time from the green country to enquire into the particulars of her daughter's death. This woman would come to me and charge me with causing the death of her child. It would be no use trying to persuade her that I had only known her daughter for a month; and she would scorn the idea of her daughter being employed as a housekeeper by a man who lived in two small rooms in a squalid little alley. What could I say? For young Emma had given me no address of any kind – not of a relative, or her employer in the City, or her friends at Chelsea. I knew of course that they would ask young Emma for her mother's address as soon as she was taken into the hospital, in case anything serious should happen. However, they would probably not use it unless they saw some sign of real danger.

These thoughts were having a bad effect on my own health; for, although I was not suffering much pain, I was still in a very weak state, and still had no power to leave my couch. It was not long before I came to the conclusion that my condition now depended on one thing – whether young Emma was alive or dead. If she lived, I too would live; if she was dead, I too must die, from having lost the will to live.

CHAPTER IX

The Pilgrimage

THE NEXT DAY, AFTER young Emma had been taken to the hospital, a woman was sent up to see me, to ask for work. I employed her immediately, as I had to have someone to look after me, being in such a helpless condition. But it did not give me much pleasure to see an old, slovenly woman standing there in the place of young Emma. There was nothing now in the way of affection, and it was all a question of money; and she came and went at her appointed hours, studied to the very minute. She was a very poor woman, with a lazy husband and a large family of little children. For that reason, I forgave her when she brought me – an invalid too – the worst kind of food and charged me the highest price for it; and when she bought large quantities of food for my bird-like picking, so that she could take food home to her youngsters. No wonder this poor woman said, when leaving me at last – 'I have worked in more than fifty different places in my time, but yours is the best I have ever had.'

At this time, when I was lying as sick as ever, and at the mercy of strangers, I received a certain letter from home, which should have been the finishing blow, but which, strange to say, knocked a new life into me – the spirit of defiance. I had already been told that a near relative of mine was on the point of death, a hundred and fifty miles away, and was commanded to come at once to her bedside. But I sent a letter back to say that I was almost in the same condition myself, and had no power to move, and hoped they would do all they could in my absence.

This second letter, which came now, when I was in this state of suffering, contained these words – 'As you are too ill to attend to matters yourself, let me inform you that a note will be sent by me to all the leading papers in the Country, to say that the mother of the well-known author —— has just died in the workhouse.' When I read these words a strange sense of humour came over me, with a strong spirit of rebellion too. 'Are all these blows, coming one after the other, from different directions, meant to kill me?' thought I. 'Whoever thinks so will be mistaken.'

With this thought I sat up on the side of the couch and reached out for my boots. But the left foot was so swollen that it was impossible to wear a boot, even in a loose state. However, I thought of my slippers, which were much too large for me, and with these I succeeded. But when I stood upright, I had no more idea of walking than a child when it is first put to stand against a chair. And when at last I did make a move, it was only to fall forward on my two hands. Not to be beaten, I persevered, and soon, with the aid of chairs and banisters, I was able to visit my room below, which my new housekeeper had just left, her duties being over for the day. To be able to do this, and to prove that I was not so helpless after all, gave me a wonderful feeling of relief and independence.

For years and years success had come to me in various forms, until I had the impression that I was a darling of the gods. For that reason, I was almost stunned at the series of blows that came on me, one after the other.

I am not what might be called a Christian man, and yet I would not care to be called an atheist. I do not like the company of unbelievers because they are loud and vulgar, and their opinions are shouted to all corners, whether we are interested or not. Not only that, but if people are happy in a certain belief, why attack it? Surely, there is no more virtue in trying to take the joy out of a man's soul than there is in taking the bread out of his mouth. However, although I am not a Christian man, I still have my own idea of a future state. It is this – that as I was hunted and pursued in this life by certain malicious people, so, in the life to follow, it is I that will be the hunter. This idea comes from no vindictive spirit, for I certainly have no desire for such a thing. It comes from the knowledge that I have never wilfully done harm to anyone, either man, woman or child. My capacity for taking punishment has been tremendous, but the spirit to inflict it on another was not given to me at birth. But in this new life to come, it will be the decree of the gods that I shall ride on the backs of my enemies, and they will live in fear of me from hour to hour. This will go on until we die again, and enter into another new state of life. For there are probably more states of life than one or two; and even in our next life to this, we will not be much wiser than we are now, to know what extraordinary life will be the end of all.

But these digressions are less likely to be welcome than the plain facts of my story. It was not long before I got someone to communicate with the hospital, and the good news came that young Emma was doing well and out of all danger. This removed my greatest fear – that I would have to give her mother an account of her daughter's life since she left home, and her death after. This good news had a wonderful effect on my body; it gave me the spirit of Lazarus, if not his strength and power, when he was told to take up his bed and walk. For I made up my mind to dress and go into the open street at the earliest opportunity, and risk what might happen. 'I will do so on Sunday,' thought I, 'when the shop below is closed and the new housekeeper has left for the rest of the day.'

When Sunday came, and I was left in the house all alone, I began to dress and was soon making my way downstairs towards the front door. But when the door was opened and I stood on the outside step, my courage almost failed me; for I felt like a young bird when he fears to leave his perch on a green bough. The air was too strong for my weak state, and I almost fell down in a swoon. However, I persevered and got away from the house, although I was staggering like a drunken man and had to rest and balance myself after every third or fourth step. It was the same feeling as I had had in the past, when I smoked tobacco after being forced to do without it for sixty days. On that occasion I had only smoked a minute or two when my brain began to swim and my knees did all they could to reach the earth and walk like feet.

When I returned to the house I had succeeded in making something like a quarter of a mile, but it had taken me half an hour to do so. Although I was tired when I got back into my room, I was happy to think that I had been out walking, and that I was no longer at the mercy of another for every little thing in life. 'Tomorrow,' thought I, 'I will do a big thing indeed: between breakfast and noon, I will walk to the Marble Arch and back, although it is a mile away. I will walk to the Marble Arch and touch it, in commemoration of my first meeting with young Emma, and to mark the return to life and health of her body and mine.'

When my new housekeeper came the next morning, she not only found me sitting at the table waiting for breakfast instead of having it in bed, but also dressed and ready to go out. It was quite clear that she did not like this sudden change, for it reminded her of the end of her service. And when I said I was going out for a walk, and felt strong enough, she sat in a chair for support and, not knowing what to say, began to abuse a certain teetotal doctor, who had not treated her with civility, all because she had had a small drop of gin and water. 'I went to consult him as a doctor, about my poor gums,' said my new housekeeper, bitterly – 'and did not expect to meet a moral crank and a teetotal maniac.'

I had never seen the poor woman in this mood before, and was glad to get away for a time. It was probably the unpleasant change in this woman that made me walk the first hundred yards with more ease than I had expected; and thinking of her made me think less of my own doings.

But although I made a good start, it was a long time indeed before I reached the Marble Arch, and I began to think I had undertaken too great a task, and should have waited another week at least. When I did reach it, at last, to touch it affectionately with my hand, I was forced to lean against it for support. It was not long before I began to realise that I would have to go into the Park and take a good rest on one of the seats before I began my return journey home. I was like a swimmer whose eagerness has taken him too far and made him forget that he has to swim the same distance back, and with less strength too. And, while I was resting in the Park, I thought of one of my own experiences, in which I had plunged into a large lake and swam so far that my companions returned to the shore frightened, to watch my small head in the far distance; and to stare until they could not trust their eyes as to whether that head was to be seen or not. But they were soon to see it slowly but surely growing larger and larger; and it was not long before I staggered out of the water, but with a whiter face than the one I had gone into it with. I had done this without a thought that a man cannot swim so far or so long in fresh water as in the salt sea. My thoughts, when I had plunged into the water, had been deep-sea thoughts, and I did not know, until it was almost too late, that the colder fresh water required more gentle thoughts.

But now things were different; for I was in a large city, with people passing by within the length of my arm: and if I had no more strength to return home with, there were thousands of people to help me, especially as I was well-dressed and had money to pay them for their time and trouble.

After I had seen and touched the Marble Arch, I was just as anxious to get back home as I had been to leave it. For I knew very well that if I rested too long in the Park my limbs would become so stiff that I would not be able to move at all. This was soon proved for, after sitting down for a quarter of an hour, I found it very difficult to walk, for the first minute or two, and the return journey took me almost twice as long. However, I reached home at last, and was very well pleased at what I had accomplished, in spite of pain and exertion. I had confidence that my strength would now increase, day by day; and although the moon might look through my window at might and see me in bed, I would never again give that chance to the midday sun.

I have already mentioned the strange behaviour of my old and new housekeeper; and how annoyed she appeared to be when she saw me dressed and heard that I was going out for a walk. Well, when I returned home, I had to put up with so much annoyance that I was very glad when her duties were over for the day, and I was left alone and in peace. For instance, when I lay on my couch helpless, and without power to move, my fire often went out for the sake of a little poking, while Mrs Larkins was in the room below. But now, when I could look after the fire myself, this wretched woman had the poker in her hand almost all the time. She poked and poked, and so viciously that the woman next door poked back at her in spite; and the both of them battled with pokers, trying to reach each other, until the noise was terrible.

'Don't trouble about the fire, Mrs Larkins,' I said, 'for I am now able to do that myself.'

These simple words seemed to make her worse, for she made another attack, and the woman next door did the same. And when she had done at last, and I was glad to get a little peace, she had not been two minutes in the room below before she came rushing up the stairs shrieking almost hysterically – 'Did you call; what can I do for you; do you want anything?'

It had been her rule, as soon as she had served my midday meal and had had her own, to sit at her own fire in the room below and have an afternoon nap. She was always in a good condition to do this, for she never forgot to charge me for a large strong drink to be taken with her meal in the middle of the day. But now, instead of sleeping quietly in the afternoon, she kept on, every quarter of an hour, shrieking from the bottom of the stairs – 'Did you call?'

In my weak condition, this sound sometimes caught me unawares, especially if I was resting and half asleep myself.

Sometimes I thought it was a cry of 'house on fire'; at other times I thought that the war was still going on, and that I was being warned by poor Louise, my former mistress, when she had burst into my room with the startled cry of 'The birds are here!' And, looking out of my window, I saw a number of the enemy's aeroplanes, in broad daylight too.

'If Mrs Larkins is in this frantic state now,' thought I, 'what will she say and do when she hears that she is no longer needed, and that my old and younger housekeeper is returning to her duties?'

But although I thought this, I had no assurance that young Emma would come back for good, even if she came back just to see me. However, of one thing I was absolutely certain – I would not have Mrs Larkins in the house any longer than I could help.

CHAPTER X

The Return

TEN DAYS HAD COME and gone since young Emma had been taken to the hospital and although I had heard on two occasions that there was no danger to her life, I was still anxious to get a letter from her own hand. It was only fair and proper that she should do this, as soon as she was able, without hearing first from me; for she had not acted towards me with honesty, nor, under the circumstances, could I have expected her to do otherwise. I suppose she had been afraid to tell me of her real condition, in fear of the consequence. For it was hardly likely that she had expected a strange and middle-aged man of the world to fall in love with her to the extent of fathering her bastard, without any knowledge of either the mother or the father. Knowing that she had left much to explain meant that she had also left something to forgive; and, not knowing the strength of my love, if I had any at all, how could she know I had a forgiving spirit? Her position was strange, and needed deep thought; and it must have puzzled her sorely as to what kind of letter she should write.

While I was busy with these thoughts, Mrs Larkins came running up the stairs in her latest manner, crying out at the top of her voice – 'Did you call, do you want anything?' How I would like to have said – 'Mrs Larkins, when I did call, you never heard me; and when I wanted anything, I often had to ask for it more than once.' But when Mrs Larkins gave me a letter and I had glanced at the handwriting, the inclination to say this passed away immediately. For I could see at once by the handwriting – childish, and done by one who was not used to writing letters – that this was not a business communication, or from any of my literary friends. The envelope was creased and crumpled, as though the writer had taken several days to write it; and had either carried it about in a pocket or slept on it after it was tucked under a pillow.

Thanking Mrs Larkins, and telling her that I did not need anything at present, I waited for that woman to leave the room. As soon as she had gone, I opened the letter and read the last words first, and saw that young Emma had signed her name. After that, I read it right through, and never before had I seen a more childish letter. With the exception of one sentence, in which she hoped that my health was improving, she said nothing more than her own experiences in the hospital. There was nothing at all about being sorry for any trouble she might have given me; and the letter ended by saying that she was 'longing to be at home again'. That she regarded my place as her home, in spite of all that had happened, and had no doubt but that she could return to it, was simplicity itself, and with all the trust of a child.

I noticed too that although she addressed me as 'Dear Mr ——,' and ended with 'Yours faithfully', above her own full name, yet, for all that, she had given her whole heart away in an unexpected quarter. For at the bottom of the letter, and tucked away in the left-hand corner, she had written one word, to stand all by itself – it was the word 'Bunnykins'. The letters in this word were much smaller and neater than the ones she had used before, and flattered me with the thought that young Emma had taken a great pleasure in writing it. With the exception of the news that she expected to be out of the hospital in ten or twelve days' time, and that she would write again, to let me know the exact date, there was nothing of more interest. But when I thought of those two words, 'home' and 'Bunnykins', I had an idea that I had found my life companion at last. However, it was a serious case, and needed more common sense than I usually had. One thought, in particular, possessed me strongly, which I would discuss with my doctor, who was due to visit me that day.

When my doctor came, he was probably very much surprised when I cut short his enquiries about my own health, and began to discuss the case of young Emma. But he had already admitted that medical treatment could do very little for me, and that the only thing that could help me was a quiet, steady life without indulgence, and to wait for time to do the rest. However, he always took a delight in spending a quarter of an hour or twenty minutes in talking of other things, especially when he had found out something about me, and made himself acquainted with some of my work. His interest became personal then, and he had too much charm to bore me: although I was too weak to allow my brain to rage like a bonfire, however interesting the subject might be. He had great tact too, for as soon as he saw that words were exciting me, he shook hands and wished me goodbye, with his usual kindly smile.

'Doctor,' I began, as soon as he was seated, and before he had time to start on another subject – 'Doctor, I have been worried very much about my little housekeeper who, as you know, is now in the hospital. First of all, I thought she might die, and I would have to give an account to her relatives, who would accuse me of her seduction, and of causing her death.'

'If I had known this, I could have relieved you of that worry at the very beginning,' answered my doctor, quickly – 'although it would have been a breach of confidence. If anyone came here with that intention, all you would have to do would have been to refer them to me, and I could have proved your innocence from her own mouth. For now, when she is out of all danger, and you, unfortunately, are not, I feel justified in making this breach of confidence. Let me tell you that the poor girl, when she first came to me for treatment, not only made a confession of her condition, but also implored me not to let you know, as she feared her dismissal.'

This news surprised me, but I had to come to the other and

more serious matter now. So I began at once, without hesitation. 'Do you know, Doctor, that she is the cause of my illness?'

'I have never once thought of that,' he answered. 'It is enough for a doctor to know that a certain disease is caught from intercourse with a woman, but it is left to the patient to say – "It is a certain woman".'

'Well, Doctor,' I continued, 'the matter stands like this. When this girl comes out of the hospital, in ten or twelve days' from now, she is coming back here to me, for as long as she cares to make this place her home. But she can only come here on one condition – that she is clean. This is as much for her own good as for my own. For instance, if she does not come here, she is not only without employment, but also without a home; and there will only be one thing left for her to do – to become a street-walker and a professional prostitute.'

'The life of the average prostitute lasts seven years,' said my doctor, with a certain amount of pity in his voice.

'If she can be saved from a life of that kind, I will do my best for her,' I said. 'I will maintain her until she gets honest employment, and give her a good start, whatever happens after. Now, what I want you to do, if you feel kindly disposed towards the both of us, is this – will you write to the hospital, saying that you think she is suffering from a venereal disease, which they may overlook?'

'I will do it at once, with pleasure,' answered my kind doctor, 'especially as I have known many cases where young girls have been in that state without knowing it. It is my impression, too, that your little housekeeper's case is one of that kind, and that she does not know her danger. But rest assured, if such is the case, she will not be allowed to go at large until all danger of infection has been removed. But if our fears are justified, you must not, of course, expect her here in ten or twelve days' time, for her treatment may take several weeks.'

'Unfortunately,' I said, 'it is all too certain, for I am here to prove it, and your own presence too. Do you know the story of the cannibal who was brought into court to serve as a witness?

When the judge said – "There is nothing to prove the death of John Summers, no grave, no stone and no monument," this cannibal pointed to his round belly and exclaimed proudly – "I am the grave; I am the stone; I am the monument." Well, Doctor, I have more proof than that to go by.'

My doctor laughed heartily at this, and said – 'Seeing that you have the courage to indulge in a grim joke, I will take advantage of that gay spirit and utter a very serious truth. Bear this in mind always: if anything like this occurs to you again, you are doomed, and nothing can help you.' There was not much need to tell me this, for I knew that the lower vitality of my advancing years could not bear the same strain again. Even now I feared that my mind was injured sufficiently to lose its full power; like a bird that is injured in the wing and tries to hop and chirp, but no longer can fly or come into full song. I had fears that this would be the case with myself as soon as I began to set my brain to make substance for a dream, or to give a solid truth the charm of a strange invention. Under these conditions, a great part of the desire to live would have gone.

My doctor's visits were now twice a week, and as my ankle was still painful and too stubborn to return to its normal size, he began to talk of a new treatment, which would last several months. But he told me frankly that although a few doctors had every confidence in that kind of treatment, he himself had none. He said that they made a great cry at a little success, but never mentioned the number of failures. When he mentioned this subject, I told him that I did not expect to be in London long enough to go through that long and expensive course; and that if my little housekeeper would join me, I intended to go into the country to live, as soon as she came out of the hospital. This was the case, as a friend of mine had already taken a house for me, and I was only waiting to see if young Emma's affection was strong enough for a quiet life in the country.

After my last meeting with my doctor, I was very anxious to see him again, to hear his news – if he had any.

'Yes,' he said, when he had come – 'I wrote to the hospital about your housekeeper's condition, but have received no answer. However, that does not matter, as they probably thought it sufficient to see into the matter, and that an answer was not necessary.'

I did not pursue this subject any further, for, although I felt that I had done the best thing, both for her and myself, yet every time I discussed her with my doctor, it seemed that I was taking away her character. The subject required delicate hands, and mine were too clumsy. It was now within two or three days of the time when young Emma, in her letter, had said that she would be leaving the hospital, and I could expect her home. But matters had changed, as I was soon to know; for her second letter came along now, not to say that she was leaving the hospital, but that she had had to undergo a second operation, and would not be able to leave for another fifteen days or more. I was very glad to hear this, for it seemed to be a proof that she was now undergoing treatment for something she had not expected, and she did not know what the second operation was for. Under these circumstances, it was a pleasure to wait for her, especially as my own condition would not allow me to leave London for another week or two.

I had already sent her some money, so that she could send out for anything she fancied that was not prohibited by the doctors; and that she might be able, knowing that she would be in a weak state, to take a conveyance from the hospital door to mine. I may as well say here that when young Emma returned she had nearly all the money I had sent her, and had spent very little. What was wanted was a parcel of food brought in by a visitor, which would have been far more acceptable than money, which she was not allowed to spend. She told me these things after, when it was too late. But we will leave that matter, and return to her third letter.

The third letter came at last, on a Monday morning, to say that she would be leaving the hospital on Thursday, and would come straight home. It was now that all my old fears came back.

Would she, no longer in fear of becoming a mother, and no longer in need of a father for her little one – would she be the same simple and affectionate girl? Would she follow me into the green country now, as fond as ever of my company? Was she coming back to me because she liked me, or because she had no other home, and needed assistance to start a new life of her own? A thousand times a day I asked myself these questions, but only one could answer them – and that was young Emma herself.

Thursday morning came at last, and I sat quietly smoking my pipe, while Mrs Larkins tidied up the room. I had not said a word to her about young Emma, or her return, preferring to let her be surprised at the last moment.

It was about ten o'clock when I heard Mrs Larkins talking to someone in the room below, and I knew that young Emma had come. She had not been driven right up to the door, as she told me afterwards, and that was the reason why I had not heard her coming.

In two or three minutes Mrs Larkins came into my room, and said, coldly and severely – 'Your old housekeeper has come, and would like to see you. Why, she is no more than a child!'

'She is older than her looks,' I answered awkwardly. 'Please tell her I am ready to see her.'

CHAPTER XI

Future Plans

WHEN YOUNG EMMA ENTERED my room, I closed the door, in case Mrs Larkins became a listener in a bend in the stairs. As soon as this was done, I took her by the hand and kissed her, and we both sat down together on the couch. She was certainly looking well after her sad experience, but I knew that the light in her eyes was not caused by good health, and was due, like the colour in her cheeks, to her excitement. I had already made up my mind not to show too much feeling, and not to go beyond a quiet and kindly civility, until I knew what young Emma intended to do. Again, I wanted to talk to her bluntly and openly of her past life, and her former lover; to know if she had any affection left for him, and if there was any danger of his interfering with her future. He might have been, for all I knew, one of those scoundrels who prey on young girls, and would think nothing of ruining her the second time; as cruel as the lightning when it strikes at eyes it has already blinded once. All I wanted to know from young Emma was this – if he still interfered with her life, when I was not near, would she let me know at once, and allow me to deal with him in my own way?

But although my mind was burning all the time with these questions, I did not think it fair or kind to mention them until the poor girl had rested for a day at least. She had already taken off her hat and coat, although she had only been in the house a few minutes, to show her trust in having come to stay. So I sat quietly, smoking my pipe, while she went on relating her hospital experiences, which were not very exciting. They were the same experiences as I had heard often before from others: the operating room, the chloroform, and then waking to find themselves in bed; and, after that, a catalogue of food and drink, and nothing more – with the exception perhaps of taking a dislike to a certain nurse or doctor. Strange to say, our soldiers, with a curious lack of imagination, were not much different; all their stories were of how they were fed, where and how they slept, and never a word about battle. They could not forget the fact that they were fed better than they had ever been before, and the larger issues of the Great War did not seem to matter. This, of course, only applies to the common soldiers, and not to the officers. But there was one experience which gave me a greater pleasure, which still clings to my memory when all the others are forgotten. One of the nurses, when passing young Emma's bed, noticed that she was crying, and wanted to know the reason why and young Emma, caught unawares, while in that weak state, answered without a second thought – 'I want to go home to Bunnykins.' The nurse assured her that she would soon be able to do so, but, seeing no improvement in young Emma's mood, thought it advisable to fetch the doctor. When the doctor came, he asked her playfully – 'Have I not been very nice to you; now, who is the man you want to see so badly?' But young Emma was not to be caught again, and, remembering that she had called me 'Bunnykins', answered – 'The gentleman I work for.'

'All in good time,' said the doctor kindly – 'all in good time. If you are a good girl, you will be able to go home soon. So, don't cry any more, or you will never get better.'

Although I had been looking forward to the time when Mrs Larkins would be leaving me for good, yet, for all that, it gave me great pleasure to offer her another week's work, while young Emma rested. Young Emma had left the hospital too soon, it seems, and against the doctor's advice. He had advised her to stay a little longer, but she had insisted on leaving. And, after she had been with me for two or three hours, and her excitement was over, it was quite obvious that she would need a few days' rest.

That night, after Mrs Larkins had gone, and young Emma and I were sitting before a cheerful fire, I thought the time had come to speak of our future plans. So I began at once – 'A friend of mine has taken a house for me in a small country town about thirty miles from London, and it is waiting until I am well enough to travel and take possession. Now, would you care to leave London and come with me?'

'Of course I'll come,' she answered quietly, as though it did not matter where she lived, as long as I was with her. She did not even ask the name of the place, nor did I think to mention it.

'We will have no friends there,' I continued, 'which will be an advantage to me – but what of you?'

'If I have my Bunnykins with me, that is all I trouble about,' answered young Emma in a simple, candid voice.

'Unfortunately, too,' I said, 'the house does not stand in its own grounds, and it will be very difficult to lead a detached life in a semi-detached house. For such near neighbours are always a nuisance; if you are not friendly enough, they do things to annoy you; and if you are friendly, there can be no more privacy. But I want to speak to you on a far more serious matter than that – it is no use making plans for the future until you have told me something about yourself.'

'What do you want to know?' she asked, without raising her eyes from her knitting, but still smiling.

'I want to know several things,' I answered. 'Who was the father of your child? Is there any danger of his interference if we lived together; and whether, if he did interfere, his old fascination would prevail? Tell me too, why he did not think you were good enough to marry, after he had ruined you!'

The last question was cruel, and meant to be, but it had the desired effect, and I was satisfied.

'Not good enough,' she exclaimed, losing her smile and her self-possession for the first time – 'not good enough indeed! The truth of the matter is this – he wanted to marry me, but I would not have him, thinking he was not good enough himself.'

The subject was delicate, and all I did after this was to keep her to it, until I had enough pieces to make the full story. This I was soon able to do, and was rather surprised at the result. It seemed to me that the case, however unfortunate it might have been for young Emma, had almost run a natural course, without any cunning designs on the man's part or folly on the woman's. Young Emma had certain friends, a mother and her daughter, on whom she used to call, when free from business. She never went to their home by appointment, but took her chances, and had never failed to find one of them at home. After she had known them for about twelve months, she met the son, a young officer in the Army, who still wore the King's uniform, although the war was now over. Now as young Emma thought she was protected by her friendship with his mother and sister, she naturally allowed him more freedom and familiarity than she would have allowed another, especially when it was in their very house and both the mother and her daughter were present. This went on for some time, until the fatal evening when young Emma called to see her friends and only found the son at home. They met at the door, surprised; he without the least suspicion of who had knocked, and young Emma without the least desire of meeting him alone. But when he explained that his mother and sister had only gone out to do a little shopping and could be expected back at any moment, she could do no other than to accept his invitation to come in and wait, which she did. The rest of the story is quite simple. If an ordinary man, in civilian's clothes, had used her too freely with his hands, she probably would have smacked his face and called him a dirty beast. But with a young officer, who had served his country and been employed in destroying her enemies, the case was different.

They had not been lovers, nor had they ever kept company together. His offer to marry her was made indifferently, with all the splendid generosity of a young officer. For that reason, as much as having no deep feeling for him, she could not accept his offer. Not only that, but the prospect of marriage did not look very bright either. He would soon be a civilian again, and would he look for work, and would he work when it was found? It was quite plain to poor Emma that his offer of marriage was not meant to be accepted.

When I sat thinking quietly of this story, it suddenly occurred to me how foolish young Emma had been, before we had both broken down. For instance, we used to have violent pillow-fights, which left us breathless and exhausted for several minutes. Not only that, but she always seemed to be doing some heavy work, bringing up a heavy chair from the room below, and taking it down again. And she never left her heavy mattress in my room, but always dragged it up the narrow stairs at night, and dragged it down in the morning. It was this strange conduct, I believe, that killed her child and brought on a premature birth. Now, the question is this – was it all done with deliberation and intention? If so, it must prove that she looked on the child as an abortion, owing to having no love or respect for the father. It gave me great pleasure to think that this might be the case. It was quite obvious to me that young Emma had no more thought of the man who had seduced her; and that the passing away of his child was less than having a tooth drawn – especially if the loss of that tooth had ruined the beauty of her face and been a serious disfigurement.

Whether we lived in the country or not, it made no difference in this – we had to leave our present rooms, for the landlord had said so; although I did not mention this to young Emma. For as soon as the woman below had informed this man of what had happened, he came to see me at once, to tell me that there was no accommodation for women, which was quite right. The man was quite civil, and explained that the place was let at a low rent because of its bad accommodation; and, although he had no objection to a woman working there in the day, he did not think it proper for one to be sleeping in.

'As you must know,' he said, 'the affair of your housekeeper interfered with my business in the shop below. But we will say no more of that; what I want to know is this – is your housekeeper coming back here, when she is well enough, to sleep on the premises?'

'Certainly,' I answered, 'if she cares to do so.' Saying this, I went on to explain that I had been looking for a better place for a long time, and would be moving as soon as I was strong enough to get about. After learning this, he left, with the same blend of business and friendliness. However, I did not mention any of this to young Emma. There was another serious reason, too, why we should leave the neighbourhood as soon as possible. Young Emma had been talked about, and now that she had come back, some of the neighbours might make it unpleasant for her. Strange to say, this thought did not seem to have ever occurred to the one whom it most concerned.

CHAPTER XII

Leaving London

THIS MOVING INTO ANOTHER house was a very serious business indeed, for, with the exception of plenty of pictures and books to cover the walls, I had no furniture worth speaking about. In fact, all I had could be contained in one small bed-sitting room. It would have been bad enough if my friend had succeeded in finding me a small cottage, but all he could find was a large eight-roomed house, and none of the rooms was small either. Under these circumstances it was a daring movement, for if it was once found out that the whole four bedrooms only contained a small cheap iron bedstead that was broken and had to be tied together with pieces of rope – if this had been found out, it would have been the talk of the whole town. However, we could manage to make the sitting room look comfortable, in case of visitors, although it would be at the expense of the rest of the house.

'All we have to do is to hang some nice curtains at the windows,' said young Emma. 'It is easy to blind the curious public,' she had said, 'by keeping the windows clean and having good blinds, and the room inside does not matter at all. That is the most important thing to do, for no one will ever find out what is behind them. I will make the curtains at once, so as to be ready to hang them.'

To this I agreed, for, strange to say, another woman had mentioned this before, years before I had met young Emma.

Young Emma was busy now, getting together a few odds and ends for our new home, cutting material to make curtains, and a hundred other little things; for we were to leave London in ten days' time. But all the business I did was to hold the cloth while she cut it, and help her to wind a little wool. Some of my readers will think this strange, seeing that I had scores of friends in London, and wonder why I was not busy in paying them farewell visits. Well, this had been my custom all through my life. Every time I left one place and went to live in another, I had always sneaked away like a thief, without wishing anyone goodbye. It was due to my shy disposition, which had always had a dread of any public display of feeling. For that reason, I have always disappeared suddenly, in case any little society I had been connected with decided to make me a presentation; or any of my friends wanted to give me a dinner that was not private enough. So that my friends never knew when I had gone somewhere else to live until my new address began to appear at the head of my letters, and the news went from mouth to mouth. One or two people, who thought that their friendship deserved more consideration, have resented this conduct of mine, so I have been told. However, I will always do the same thing, no matter how long I live in a place, and no matter how friendly the people are; for I act according to my strange disposition, and it is the only natural thing for me to do.

Up to the present I had not given young Emma much money at one time, but now the hour came to fulfil a certain promise; so that I was not surprised to hear her ask, one evening – 'When are you going to give me the five pounds you promised me, to spend on myself?'

'You can have it at once,' I answered, taking out my pocket book and counting five one pound notes into her hand. She was very pleased to get them, which was probably the largest sum she had ever had of her own.

That same evening she began to mention the number of things that were needed, in the way of sheets, blankets, a quilt, and several carpets and mats. When I heard this, I said – 'When I go to the bank in the morning, I will draw enough money to get some of those things. But we are not very rich, and we must furnish the house bit by bit, when we are in it, and as I make more money.'

When I returned from the bank the next morning, I gave young Emma another ten pounds; so that she now had fifteen pounds in her possession, counting her own. But when I saw her leaving the house, I was filled with a sudden fear. 'This will be a strong test of her honesty and affection,' thought I – 'and I would not be at all surprised if I never saw her again. If she has any objection to leaving London, or the least idea that she could do better with her life than to live with me – now will be the test. Fifteen pounds is, to her, a large sum indeed; and if she comes back, I shall know that it will be through her affection for me, and be better satisfied than I have been for a long time.'

Young Emma was going all the way to Camden Town, where a certain firm had a great sale on, and were selling things at a low price. So that, in spite of riding the best part of the journey there and back on an omnibus, it would still take her more than an hour before she could get back home. But when that hour had come and gone, and Emma had not returned, I began to fear for the worst. It was not the money that worried me, although I could ill afford to lose so large a sum; what upset me most was the destruction of my new dreams. If she had gone for good, I would have to remain in my present squalid surroundings, for I would not have the courage to live alone in a strange, country village.

And what dreams I had had too, of passing more trees than human beings, and hearing more birds than human voices. Even the night before I had seen, in my dreams, a tree heavy with red cherries, and flaming in a meadow. And while I looked, every cherry turned into a little red bird, and the leaves became wings. Then all at once all those little red birds flew up, like one, higher and higher, while they disappeared in the Heavens, like Elisha of old, when he went up in a chariot of fire.

But just as I had given up all hope of seeing young Emma again, I was suddenly relieved by hearing her coming up the stairs.

'You have been gone nearly two hours,' I said, quietly, not caring for her to know anything of my worry or suspicion.

'Yes,' she answered – 'I took the wrong omnibus, and did not know it until I found myself at the Old Bailey.'

The morning came at last, when we were to leave London, with every hope that our happiness would continue in another, and more pleasant place. At nine o'clock a small motor-van was at the door, to take our few goods and chattels into the country. We ourselves were going by rail, from Victoria, and would be at the new house when the furniture arrived, early in the afternoon. We trusted everything to the van, and, with the exception of a small light bag to hold one or two things that I treasured most, we had nothing to encumber us or to need our care during the journey.

The ride to Victoria was not very cheerful, and we scarcely uttered a word all the way. Young Emma spent her time looking through the window at the various shops we were passing, and the dresses worn by her own sex. What depressed me more than anything was that I did not know her thoughts, whether she was happy at leaving London, or miserable. I began to wonder too if she had any misgiving at going to live alone in the country with a man she had only known for a short time. For if I did not treat her kindly, it would be much easier for her to leave me when in London than in a small country town. Thinking of this, I thought it would be wise to reassure her at the earliest opportunity. So that we had no sooner stepped into an empty railway carriage, before the arrival of other passengers, than I put my arm around her waist and kissed her. The result was good indeed, for her face brightened at once. And when the train was in the green country, and I looked sideways at young Emma's face, the sight of the green woods and the open meadows seemed to please her more than the shops in London.

'She will love the green country, of course,' thought I – 'for has she not already told me that she is a farmer's daughter? The only fear she can have, if she has any at all, is a change in her lover – from kindness to neglect and cruelty.'

CHAPTER XIII

The Green Country

THE HOUSE WE WENT to live in consisted, as I have said before, of eight rooms, and was semi-detached. A little house of four rooms, and standing in its own grounds, would have pleased me much better, especially if the rooms had plenty of breathing space. It may be necessary for a king or emperor to live in a palace whose windows number the days in a year, because of his large household and public receptions. But as a lonely man of dreams, I would be quite satisfied if my windows numbered the months that are in a year, and I only had the choice of two small doors to come and go.

However, the house was well-situated, and had a small narrow lawn at the side, with a row of six large trees overlooking a high wall. At the back was a large garden with fruit trees, shrubs and evergreens, flowers, and a summer-house in a sunny corner. This garden interested me as much as the inside of the house interested young Emma. For while she was indoors, looking at the rooms, I was in the garden, trying to name the trees, and thinking of their summer glory, for it was now October. And what a dream of leaves I had: I wanted to cover the whole house all over with green leaves; around every window, all over the roof, and even around the chimney stack. But this, of course, would take years and years; and life would be generous indeed, if I ever saw that done.

As soon as we were settled in our new home, it was necessary for me to get another doctor, for I still suffered from my complaint and my ankle still refused to let me walk for more than a quarter of an hour or twenty minutes. This doctor no sooner came than he proposed a course of inoculation, which would last three months, to which I agreed. 'It is not very painful,' he said, 'and there is no danger – although you may feel a bit feverish for an hour or two after each inoculation.'

But the truth is this – I felt so feverish after each visit that I was afraid I would either go mad or die. At the end of this treatment, I found myself no worse and no better than at the beginning. So, after I had paid my bill, I made up my mind to see another doctor, and to be wily in the way I approached him. For it suddenly occurred to me that the rheumatism in my ankle was due to my venereal complaint and, if I was cured of the latter, the other would go away. My rheumatism was due to poisoned blood, and not caused by old age or a constitution weakened by a hard life of exposure in the open air. 'My next doctor's bill will be the fourth,' thought I – 'and it must be the last.'

These thoughts had no sooner taken possession of my mind than I went to see another doctor and told him of my complaint, which had lasted several months. 'What have you been doing for it?' he asked, after an examination.

When I told him, he said – 'You have been doing the right thing, but you have not done it thoroughly and properly, and that is why you are not cured. It seems to me that your doctor should have known this, after all this time. Can you come here tomorrow evening, at the same time, and we'll see what can be done.'

'By the way,' I said, as though it were an afterthought – 'by the way, I suffer from a little rheumatism too, and, after this thing is over, I would like you to treat me for that.'

'Very well,' he answered, 'but when this affair is cleared up, I don't suppose there will be any more rheumatism.'

This was the same conclusion as I had come to myself, and I was delighted to hear a doctor say the same thing. When I left him I was full of hope that something would be done at last. The result of my second consultation with my new doctor was good, so he said. It consisted of a quarter of an hour's massage, and then my own treatment. The latter I had not done properly, he said, and showed me how to do it.

'If this had gone on much longer,' he said, 'it would have led to a serious surgical operation, but I am hopeful now that it will not be needed.'

When I heard this, I was considerably alarmed, for I had never realised that there was as much danger as that. In fact, I had been under the impression that if I cared to wait long enough, time would have purified my blood and brought back my health, without a question of doctors at all.

After this I paid him three more visits, and went through the same treatment, and that was not only the end of my venereal disease but also the end of my rheumatism.

We had now been living in the country for several months, and my health had not allowed me to travel far from home. Strange to say, I had not the least inclination to return to London, not even for a day. There appeared to be no ending to my liking for nature; whether a tree was so leafy that it reduced the whole heavens to a few blue eyes, or whether the twigs were as thin and bare as the bird's legs that used them – it was all the same to me.

We were now busy planting here and there in the garden; so that the following summer should have such a blaze of colour that I hoped to have as my guests not only hundreds of bees and butterflies but also the great dragon-fly, with his crowned head, and his breast covered with shining honours.

As for young Emma, she had a green hand; for everything she planted in the garden grew and came to leaf, and reached the age of blossom – nothing seemed to die. The piece of ivy I tore from a wild bank and brought home was planted by young Emma, and showed two new leaves in less than a month, yet it was all done out of season. But the piece of ivy at its side, which had been planted carefully by a skilled gardener, at the proper time, had never shown any life at all, and had withered and died.

At this time I was very happy, and felt sure that my complaint had gone at last. On my doctor's advice, I was to make a certain test every day, for about two weeks; and if, at the end of that time, the test held good, I could have every confidence that I was all right. This I did and, being thoroughly satisfied with the result, I celebrated the occasion by drinking half a bottle of wine. It was a glorious celebration for a drinking man, to whom drink had been forbidden for several long months.

Young Emma would not have been a very good companion for the ordinary literary man, and yet she pleased me well enough. It did not worry me in the least to be asked suddenly, when my brain was struggling with what some people would call 'lofty thoughts' – 'Why is a bar of soap like the Bible?' She was fond of riddles, and I was not good at solving them, to her joy. And when she asked me one evening, in her simple, childish way – 'Are you as great as Shakespeare, Bunnykins?' I did not think it worthwhile to take a too modest view of the matter, and answered her in the same simple way – 'Sometimes.'

Her questions sometimes fed my imagination, and had a peculiar interest to me as a literary man. This was one: 'Suppose a man had come up to you when in your thirtieth year, and said – "Your wife has just been born"; would you have believed him?' Or – 'Did it ever occur to you, when you were thirty years old, that your future wife was only a small baby, and you would have to wait until she was a woman before you could marry her?'

I always tried to give some pleasant answer to these strange questions, knowing what pleasure it gave her in asking them.

No, young Emma was not a brilliant talker, by any means; but it was restful and soothing to feel one's self in the presence of a great heart and an affectionate spirit, and not a great brain. For that reason, our language was often nothing more than cuddles and kisses, and making love in silence; in the same way as I would hold a flower by its stalk and bend down to smell it, without a word to follow.

Strange to say, I had never wanted anyone to share my literary dreams; and that is why young Emma, not being interested in them, suited me so well as a companion. When I gave her a book that was written by myself, all she did was to take a knife and cut the leaves carefully. After doing this, she kissed its cover, and then kissed me, before she placed it among her own books, to be read – any time.

CHAPTER XIV

The Quarrel

FOR TWO OR THREE weeks I was in splendid spirits, for I now felt certain that my blood was made pure, and my full health must come back in consequence. It was now that I began to think seriously of making a straightforward proposal to young Emma, to fix, if she approved of it, a special day for our marriage. It would have to be quiet and not talked about; for I had an idea that it was suspected in the neighbourhood that she was my mistress as well as my housekeeper. And, although young Emma was as indifferent to her reputation as I was to my own, yet for all that, I came to the conclusion that a woman needed protection, whether she thought so or not. So I proposed to young Emma, in a quiet, simple way, and was accepted. Without any shyness or questions of any kind, she answered 'yes', as though she had expected the question for a long time, and was not surprised when it came at last.

We had now been engaged for two weeks, and the marriage was to be at a Register Office, in a month's time. But this happiness was not to last long, for I had no sooner co-habited with her, after I felt positive that my complaint had gone, than I was to receive another shock – it was either the return of the old complaint or the catching of a new one. If it was the latter, the case was serious indeed, and was likely to lead to my death, and before long too. It proved too that young Emma was still suffering from that complaint. For the first time I felt a certain amount of bitterness towards her. To think that I had been under the care of several doctors, and that she, who was the cause of my illness, had taken no steps to make herself clean, filled me with bitter thoughts. And yet I could not understand how she, if such were the case, could keep going without any apparent suffering or inconvenience. This was a mystery to me. However, I said nothing at the time, but thought it was wise to see my doctor first, and hear what he had to say.

That very evening, following my horrible discovery, I consulted my doctor again, and underwent an examination. When he saw a small sore, about the size of a pin's head, his face became grave indeed, and he said – 'Until there is some development, I cannot say anything definite. But if it is what I fear, you are in for a long and dangerous illness. On the other hand, it may pass away in a day or two, and be of no consequence whatever.'

When I heard these words I was considerably alarmed, and feared the worst. It must be remembered that I had never had a sore on my body before, not a pimple, a boil or tumour; only an occasional clean cut from the careless use of a knife or razor. Under these circumstances, no wonder I was afraid; and no wonder I could not look straight into young Emma's face.

When the evening began to wear on towards bedtime, I could contain myself no longer, and said to young Emma, assuming a calmness that I did not feel – 'I am afraid we will have to postpone our marriage, because my old complaint has come back. I don't think it would be wise for us to marry yet, until my health is better – and you, of course, must see to your own.'

What young Emma thought of the last part of my sentence, which was meant to give her a strong hint, I cannot say. As far as I could see, the words did not seem to have any meaning for her. But her poor little white face twitched so much, and looked so weak and pathetic, that I could hardly refrain from taking back my words – although I knew it was not wise to mince matters any longer. That she suffered acutely from my words, I could see, but she said nothing at all in answer to them. She only sat looking into the fire, until her face, getting under her control, became hard and set. And as she did not make any answer, I did not say any more, but opened a book and began to read. But the silence was so terrible that I sometimes felt inclined to cry out aloud, to prove that there were two human bodies in the room, and not two spirits. I lit my pipe a score of times, not for the sake of smoking, but to make a little sound that, translated into words, would say – 'We are not dead yet.'

Although we had said so little, or, to be correct, I had said so little – for she had said nothing at all – yet, for all that, it was clear that there was a misunderstanding, and that we had quarrelled. So, when our bedtime came and she was waiting for me to light the candle, she, not seeing me make any movement to do so, said – 'It is ten o'clock.'

'Very well,' I answered, 'you must go to bed alone tonight, for I have work to do and must sit up late.'

What she thought of this I cannot say, for she still had no answer to anything I said. However, she got up and lit the candle herself, for the first time, and went to bed alone, for the first time too. And when she left the room, she did not say 'Goodnight', neither did I.

What did our two animals think of this strange conduct? The dog, Beauty Boy, who had been accustomed to follow us both upstairs, and slept on a mat outside our bedroom door, seemed to show a certain amount of distress. For as soon as he saw young Emma with the lighted candle, then he followed her to the door. But when he looked back and saw no movement on my part, he stood in the open doorway, irresolute; first looking after her, and then looking back at me. When I saw this, I caught him by the collar and pulled him gently back into the room, and then closed the door.

But what of the cat – what of my black Venus of a cat? There she lies – the strangest creature I have ever known. When I played with her this morning, her eyes were all yellow, with the exception of two pupils that were no more than two thin lines that were hardly seen. But when I look at her now, the pupils are large, round, black balls, and the yellow circles are as thin as an old woman's ring. At the present moment her eyes are wild and bulging, and she appears to have more knowledge than the dog of what has happened. It had always been my custom to take this black Venus of a cat into the kitchen, just before ten o'clock; where, after I had given her a last saucerful of milk, she remained till morning. But on this particular night, she not only did not appear in a hurry to go, but sat looking at me with two large wild eyes, defiantly, it seemed, as much as to say – 'Be the tyrant still, for I refuse to move, and will have to be carried.' This is the first time she has ever failed to show me some affection at night. Seeing that cat crouched on the arm of a chair and looking at me with those two glaring eyes did not make me feel comfortable. So I carried her into the kitchen, gave her her milk and left her. After which I returned to the sitting room, and sat down to think, and think, and think.

It is now midnight, and the hour is quiet and still. There is no sound heard, except the voices of my neighbour's pigeons. I think the violin is the most wonderful instrument that was ever invented, and to be its master is to be a remarkable man. But what master could express the tenderness in the voice of a dove or a pigeon? These thoughts pass away quickly, and I am wondering whether I am doing the proper thing with the affectionate little creature who is alone upstairs. In the end, I am asking myself this question – 'Must I go upstairs and kiss her, because she is simple, fond and affectionate, and forgive her for bringing me to an early death? And yet, what else can I do? She does not seem to know the dangerous state she is in, and has no knowledge of disease. Although my illness is a mystery to her, she never doubts but what it is as respectable as indigestion or lumbago.'

In spite of all my thinking, I could make no definite plans for the future. If the doctor was right in his fears, that my complaint had developed into a more dangerous state, that would lead to madness and an early death – what was I to do about young Emma, who was the cause of it all?

She had always said that she would never leave me, no matter what happened. If I drove her away, she would come back; and if I left her, she would follow and not rest until she had found me. And when I mentioned, with my greater knowledge of life, how easy it was for a man to drive a woman away, without threatening her or laying his hands on her, but by simply nagging at her every day from morning till night – when I came to this part, young Emma had laughed heartily, and said – 'But you are the wrong kind of man to do that. If you want to use your tongue that way, you will have to give up smoking tobacco, and I am sure that will never happen.'

I was not much surprised at hearing these words, for it had always been obvious that young Emma had no fear of me. Although I had, on one or two occasions, burst out with vulgar words, like a bully, which all men who are born of the common people are apt to do, in spite of their later association with people of more culture – although I had done this, once or twice, it seemed to give her more amusement than distress or fear. Perhaps the reason is this – that she also came of the common people, and their blunt words and open anger were natural to her.

I remember telling young Emma, one day, how I got into trouble with a London cabman, and the result. At that time I was crossing the Thames Embankment at Charing Cross, and walked in front of his horse, so that he had to pull up sharply. And when he called me a foul epithet, I returned it with another; and it was not long before we were abusing each other in the worst language we could think of. Unfortunately for him, I had a large assortment of American oaths to add to my English ones, and was soon getting the better of him. But we had not been using this strong language for many minutes when I suddenly felt a pat on the shoulder, followed by a sweet, encouraging voice, which said – 'That's right, give him hell! Give the old swine double hell!' When I heard this, my power of abuse failed me at once, for I was not doing it for the amusement of others; and the old cabman seemed to have the same thought too, for he applied the whip to his horse and drove away. So we both left the young lady standing there, disappointed at the sudden end to a terrific argument. When I told young Emma of this incident, she thoroughly enjoyed it. In fact, I have heard her, more than once, use bad language herself; but the words lacked variety and there was no solid emphasis.

But we will let that go for, at the present time, the feeling between young Emma and myself was too serious for bad language. On my part, it was a question of whether our love should continue if there was no prospect of my body getting well; and on her part it was disappointment that her love had received an unexpected check. The matter was serious, but she did not know it. In two or three days from now, I would know more; and, if it came to the worst, young Emma and I must part company. What the poor girl would say to that, I did not know. But when I tell her the cold facts, and explain how impossible it will be for our affection to continue, under the strange conditions, we may be able to make some sad but wise arrangement for our future life, which must not be together.

It was now after midnight, and I went into the garden for a few minutes, before going to bed. But when I got there I found that it was not only raining, but there was a little lightning too, and a very faint rumble of thunder in the distance. When I saw this, it reminded me at once that young Emma was afraid of lightning and thunder, and dreaded to be alone whenever there was a storm of that kind. However, this was only the beginning, and it was hardly likely that she, in a room with the windows almost closed, would know of this storm, until it came nearer home.

While I stood there, feeling the light rain, and waiting to see the occasional flash of light, my thoughts were still of the young girl who was now all alone in the house, and, fortunately, was not aware of it. 'There,' thought I, looking into the heavens, 'there we see water and fire at play, and neither can extinguish the other. In the same way the light of love can no more be blotted out by tears than the lightning can be blotted out by a deluge of rain.'

I was reminded now of a little poem that I had found in an anthology. As it was very small and appropriate to young Emma's life and mine, I had committed it to memory. In quoting it, I make no claims for any merit it might have, and only say that it was found in the best lyrical company, which may be a mistake or not. It is called *Storms*.

She fears not me:
  Neither my thunder,
Nor my lightning, startles her –
  To make surrender.

But when my friend
  In Heaven makes thunder –
Her spirit breaks, and turns
  To fear and wonder.

Lightning and thunder,
  Give her no rest:
Bring her head back again –
  Back to my breast.*

But when, after a little difficulty, I had got this poem right, for my memory is not very good – I began to notice that the lightning had received more body, and the thunder had become a voice itself, and no longer a faint echo. And it now occurred to me that although young Emma had probably lost her affection for me, yet, for all that, it was not right to leave her there all alone, knowing how much she feared this same lightning and thunder. My presence would certainly calm her fears, even if it did not

* 'Storms' was in fact written by Davies himself, and appeared in *The Poet's Calendar*, published by Cape in 1927.

bring back her love. I was reminded too of the lateness of the hour by my fine mongrel Beauty Boy, who began to rub against me, and who was always jealous of long thoughts. And when he saw me going towards the door, he wagged his tail and led the way, looking backwards all the time.

It was not long before I was in the bedroom, undressing, and it was all done very quietly. Young Emma was fast asleep, and she had not yet heard the thunder, it seems. She was at the far side of the bed, with her back turned towards me, to show that we had quarrelled. But in spite of all my attempts to be quiet, I had no more than half undressed than I stumbled against the bed and shook it violently. The result of this was that young Emma made a sudden start, and turned her face towards me; and, although she was now wide awake, and saw it was me, she did not turn her back again – why? A most horrible thought possessed me. I thought that young Emma had not been to sleep at all and, hearing my accidental movement, got the impression that I had come to murder her. For although she was facing me now, with her eyes closed, she was lying there so quiet that I knew she had made her body almost breathless, so that her ears could be of more value to her than the corners of her eyes. It was a most horrible thought to have, for I, of course, had never once had the least intention of doing her any harm. The only likelihood there was of my doing that would be if I went mad, and did what all mad people do – attack the one I loved most.

But whatever young Emma's thoughts had been, it soon became clear that her fear of lightning and thunder was much greater than her fear of me. For as soon as I got into bed, she began to creep closer and closer; and it was not long before she was close enough to make the quickest movement I have ever seen her make. There had come a great clap of thunder, just as I was in the act of yawning, with my arms outstretched; and before that peal was over, young Emma had not only tucked her head under my arm, but had also nuzzled close to my breast. It was quite obvious from this, when she took such a quick advantage of my outstretched arms, that young Emma was not half asleep, neither was she drowsy.

But although she lay there until the storm was over, and our two bodies needed a different position, no conversation passed between us. It was in the morning, when she said – 'How the lightning frightened me last night, and the thunder too! But when I saw you lying at my side, with an arm outstretched, like Christ on the Cross – I took shelter at once, and all my fears were gone.'

CHAPTER XV

The Fur Coat

THE NEXT MORNING, IT was very quiet, after the storm; not only in nature, but also in two human breasts. But the quiet of nature was not so deceptive as the human quiet, for young Emma and I had not ended our quarrel, in spite of the thunderstorm, and only a few cold words passed between us. As far as I was concerned, reconciliation seemed to be impossible. The hand of doom was on me, I believed; for, after twenty-four hours, I still saw no improvement in my state, and, until I did, I could not treat her in a more friendly spirit. As for young Emma, she did not appear to realise the great danger I was in, or expected to be in before many days had passed. Although I had told her what the doctor had said, that I was likely to be in for a long and serious illness, and hinted at madness and an early death – she did not appear to know what I meant, and probably thought that now was the time when her affection would be needed most, and that she would never forsake me in my trouble. She was either very callous or very innocent, and I preferred to think it was the latter. When I suggested that she should see a doctor, she asked – 'Why, what can I say to him?' When I heard this, I could say no more, and thought to myself – 'She will find out for herself before long, and the matter must wait until then.'

Now it happened that just about this time a certain letter came, which I had expected for a long time. It was young Emma's custom to pick up all letters, as they came – and I let her do so on this occasion. As there was an imprint on the envelope, and young Emma knew I expected a cheque, and from whom, it was not many minutes before she said – 'You promised me a ten guinea fur coat, as soon as you had the money. Can I go up to town for it tomorrow morning?'

When I heard this, I did not know what answer to make, for I did not want her to go all the way to London unless we were more friendly towards each other. But I had promised her faithfully that she should have a fur coat as soon as this cheque had come, and there was no plain reason why I should break my word.

'Are you going up for the whole day?' I asked, in a matter-of-fact way, wondering if she would have one thought that I would be left alone to see the baker, butcher and others, and get my own meals too. As a bachelor I had done this often, and thought nothing of it; but I did not expect to find that indifference in a girl who professed to love me, and waited for her answer with a little anxiety.

'No, no,' she answered, impulsively – 'I would not leave my Bunnykins all that time by himself. A train leaves here at eleven o'clock and reaches London at twelve fifteen. In three quarters of an hour I shall have the coat and be back at London Bridge Station in time to catch the one o'clock train, which reaches here at two fifteen. At half past two I shall be back home again, with my Bunnykins and a fur coat.'

'But you will not have time for the midday meal,' I said.

'I'll try to find time for a cup of tea and a bun,' she answered; 'if I can't, it does not matter.'

After these few words we spent a quiet evening. I noticed, while she was knitting industriously, that she was smiling to herself all the while. But my thoughts did not make me smile; they were too sad for that.

The next morning young Emma was up early, although she had hours to catch her train. But the morning was wet, and when the time came for her to leave the house, the rain came so fast and heavy that it could not reach the drain-holes quick enough, and made streams in the gutter.

'Surely you are not going to town in weather like this,' I said, 'and will wait till tomorrow; or, if you are so eager to possess the coat, why not go up by a later train?'

But young Emma was determined to go by that train, and nothing could persuade her to the contrary. She was so determined to go that she busied herself in different parts of the house, where my voice could not reach her with clear words. And when the time of parting came at last, she gave me one short hasty kiss and left without another word. However, there was nothing unusual in this haste, for I always had all I could do to prevent Beauty Boy from following her, and it was the same on this occasion.

It is generally thought that bachelors are selfish men, and that is why they do not marry – but this is not always the case. In my own case, it was only a matter of maintaining another, and keeping two people in comfort, instead of one, that kept me from marriage until late in life. And as I did not marry when very poor, with too much thought for a woman to do that, so the only reason why I have not kept a dog before now is because of my great love of dumb animals. I would never think of keeping a dog, or, for that matter, any other animal, unless I could give it close and proper attention; and it is only as a married man that I am able to do that. My life has been in danger on several occasions, but I have always counted my adventure with a certain strange dog as one of my most trying experiences. This was in the wilds of America, when I had to threaten a dog for over ten minutes, to prevent him from becoming more friendly and making me his master. Under the circumstances, I persuaded myself that I acted wisely for the both of us, in giving the poor creature a chance to find a more prosperous master.

It was my usual habit to walk for about two hours every morning, after which I seldom went out again during the rest of the day. Beauty Boy always accompanied me, and followed me all over the house, after breakfast, for fear I should go without him. But on this occasion, when young Emma had gone to town, we were almost an hour late, and the dog could not understand why his master was still in his slippers, and without his cap and stick. Knowing that I was now confined to the house, because of several people that were expected to call, I led the way into the garden, and around the house, hoping that Beauty Boy would get tired of waiting and go off on his own account. But the poor creature would not do so and, when I came back into the house, he still followed close behind me.

'What are we going to do now, Beauty Boy?' I asked, with something lumpy in my throat, as I stroked his head while he lay on the floor looking disappointed and sad. 'What are we going to do now, Beauty Boy; left here alone and forsaken by the one who looked after us? Unless she comes back, I shall sell up everything and become a wanderer again, and you and I will have to part company, I fear. It was not fair to bring you here to share two lives that were so uncertain, and so likely to change. We were selfish creatures to do that, Beauty Boy.'

Yes, I felt certain now, the more I thought the matter over, that young Emma had gone for good. I was so convinced of this that I was already wondering what I would do and where I would go. It was the dog and the cat that worried me most, and I cursed myself for allowing these poor creatures to give me their trust and affection while my life and home were too unsettled to receive them. There were several things that seemed to prove that young Emma would not return. In the first place, our little quarrel had not helped our love, by any means. Again, why did she insist on going to town in all this rain, when any other day would have done just as well? And, if I was not satisfied with our life together, was she not free to go away, before our marriage made it more difficult? It must be remembered too that I had given her eleven guineas, ten guineas for a fur coat, and one guinea for travelling expenses. In addition to this, she had about two pounds towards housekeeping. When I considered all this – our quarrel, her full purse, and her freedom to do what she liked – when I thought of all this, I felt certain that I had seen the last of young Emma.

'This ought not to have happened,' I thought, 'for it is going to be very difficult to live without her.'

What made me suffer more, and regret what had happened, was the discovery that not a sign remained of my complaint, and that the doctor's fears and mine were groundless; and that he was right, when he had said – 'It may pass away in a day or two, and be nothing of any consequence.' Yes, it had passed away – but I had quarrelled with Emma and probably lost her for ever, and there had been no real cause.

When the time came for the midday meal, I fed the animals, but did not eat anything myself. However, I drank a large glass of strong wine, and the effect on my empty stomach was to make me as drowsy as the two animals, when they had settled down after their own full meal. The more I thought of these two animals, the more my sorrow increased. Beauty Boy, would, according to the nature of a dog, follow his master to the ends of the earth, that was certain; where my home was, there his would be. But my black Venus of a cat would, according to the nature of a cat, be more faithful to her home than to her master; and, although I forced her to go away with me, she would soon be lost, when she had her liberty, in her effort to find her way back to the old home. The cat was now asleep, enjoying the comfort of a good fire and a thick, soft rug. But the dog was beginning to show some distress, and pricked his ears several times, as he looked towards the front door; but it was only the sound of my next door neighbour, or strangers passing in the street outside.

When the church clock struck the half hour at two thirty, and young Emma had not returned, I knew the worst; and all my interest in the home had gone. 'It is all over now,' I thought, taking off my slippers and throwing them down, to put on my boots for walking out – 'it is all over now, and no matter who comes knocking at the door, let them knock, go or wait.'

But I had scarcely uttered these words when Beauty Boy suddenly cocked his two ears, one after the other, and the next instant leapt across the room and stood motionless behind the door. I had heard nothing, although my hearing is good, and not many sounds escape me. However, he was right this time, for I was soon to hear a sharp, little rat-tat on the knocker, and my heart bounded with the glad cry – 'It is young Emma!'

Yes, it was young Emma, sure enough, proud and happy, and wearing her little ten guinea fur coat, which became her very well indeed. Although I tried to keep a restraint on my feelings, some of it must have escaped in the reception I gave her, for she asked, after I had kissed her – 'Are you glad I have come back?'

'Beauty Boy appears to be glad enough,' I answered, laughing, and evading her question.

But the cat had only half opened her lazy eyes to see what all the commotion was about; and then, tightening the curl in her body, to shut out further disturbance, was soon gone back into her heavy slumber.

CHAPTER XVI

The Marriage

AFTER WHAT HAPPENED IN the last chapter, my suffering in thinking young Emma had left me, I felt very pleased to think I was to marry her in a few more days. For although I had mentioned a postponement, which seemed to give her much pain and disappointment, yet, for all that, I had done nothing at the Register Office to alter my original plan. It was another proof of her affection that she, as a single girl and free to do what she liked, had come back to her lover. She could have left me without any trouble on her conscience that she had not acted honestly; for the money I had given her was, after all, no more than her salary as a housekeeper, and there had never been any question of paying her that. But the most extraordinary thing of all was that she had no fear, in spite of what I had said of my complaint leading to madness and, perhaps, a violent and early death. It was probable that she could not visualise this state in my particular person, seeing that she had never seen me other than calm and good-tempered.

However, all danger of that was now removed, and we could look forward to a merry Christmas together, which was close at hand. And then, following close on Christmas, we were to be married quietly at a register office. These two events, the first with its appeal to all, and the second with its special appeal to ourselves, gave us enough to think about for the next twenty-four hours.

I was amazed to see how much of a child young Emma was as soon as she began to make preparations for Christmas. On

Christmas morning the mantelpiece was like a cattle market, stocked with horses and cows made of chocolate, with sheep and fat pigs made of white sugar. Long chains of coloured paper were hanging from the highest corners, which I thought only the spiders and flies could reach. Here and there I saw large gorgeous parasols and fans, with pretty lanterns too; while from the ceiling hung large balloons, round, oval and sausage-shaped. Everywhere I looked I saw either a quaint little man or woman, or a young cherub, or boxes covered with silver tinsel, which contained – but that was young Emma's secret, and was only to be known at a certain time. It was the most gorgeous room I had seen in my life, and yet it was all built up with odd pennies, this cost twopence-halfpenny, and that cost a penny more, and two or three things cost sixpence each. But the whole amount together did not exceed a pound, I swear. The effect was rich indeed, and I soon learnt that young Emma had been getting these things together in secret for some time past, to give me a Christmas Eve of surprise and wonder. But the greatest surprise of all was to come on Christmas morning; for we had both bought each other a number of presents, with so much generosity that we had to use pillow-slips to hold them, our stockings not being large enough. These pillow-slips were kept in a secret place and, as soon as we were in bed at night, and I had blown out the light, we were to exchange them in the dark. After that they were to be opened in the morning, and she had to thank me with a kiss for every present I made her, and I was to do the same for hers. All this was done according to plan – except that young Emma woke at daybreak and insisted on the pillow-slips being opened at once. Unfortunately, at this moment, our neighbour's cockerel began to crow in such a horrible voice that young Emma said – 'That poor bird has a severe cold.' There was certainly something wrong with the bird, for Beauty Boy, who slept outside our bedroom door, barked furiously – a thing he had never done before at that early hour in the morning. As it was impossible to sleep again, while this noise was going on, we decided to open our pillow-slips. Some of the presents had a great welcome, and there was not one that caused the least disappointment.

My Christmases in the past had not been very happy, with the exception of those that came in my childhood and in my youth. As I had no home of my own, I was beholden to strangers for their kindness in making me one of their own family at Christmas time; and they did the service so well that I must always remain grateful to them for their efforts to make me comfortable and happy. But at the bottom of my heart I realised my lonely position in the world, and longed for the power to do for others even as these kind friends were doing for me. And now that time had come, at last; for I had a nice little home of my own, with young Emma in charge. Under these changed conditions in my life, I will leave the reader to guess whether I was happy or not. At this time we had very little money, for we had been so eager to furnish the house that I had spent money thoughtlessly, without thinking of the future. Not only that, but certain strange bills came in, which took me by surprise. I had bought the house for two hundred pounds, and there was a mortgage of eight hundred pounds left. The result of this was that I not only had to pay income tax on the house – which really had nothing at all to do with my earnings – but also had to pay rates and taxes, in addition to the interest on my mortgage. Repairs had to be done too, and I was responsible for it all. In fact, I had to pay for everything in connection with this house, and yet I only owned one-fifth of it; other people seemed to profit by my investment, and all I had was the honour of being called a landlord, and the worry of examining my property every day, to give it support every time it threatened to fall down.

A few days after Christmas young Emma and I were married quietly at a register office and, after leaving, had the midday meal at a restaurant, returning home to tea and dinner as man and wife. The only unusual thing we did, to celebrate the occasion, was to have a second Christmas dinner at night – a more elaborate meal than we had accustomed ourselves to. What young Emma thought of this – a marriage without a honeymoon – I cannot say, but she appeared to be very happy as it was. There had been enough money to spend on new clothes and creature comforts, and she did not seem to trouble about leaving home, or going to theatres. However, I promised her a holiday before long, as soon as I had the money to spare, and we would make that holiday our honeymoon as well.

In thinking of my simple marriage with young Emma, I was reminded of another wedding, to which I had been invited some years before. On that occasion the bride and bridegroom were so rich in presents that it was thought advisable to have a plain-clothes detective from London to watch over them, and to keep a sharp eye on the numerous guests. After the ceremony the happy couple left for a month's travel on the Continent of Europe. But in less than six months after this great triumph their happiness had gone, and it is only the child that came along that keeps them together now.

But my simple marriage with young Emma would not end like that, I felt sure. For we were happy in one another, and did not need presents or anything else. In fact, we had nothing in the house to give us amusement, only the bonbons, which let off a sharp report when we both pulled; and which contained riddles, paper-caps and trinkets. But I am wrong in saying that there was nothing in the house to give us amusement, for I had forgotten the mongrel, Beauty Boy, and the black Venus of a cat. There was enough amusement in watching the behaviour of these two, when the bonbons made their sharp report; and when young Emma and I looked unfamiliar to them in our strange paper-caps, which we changed and changed, each time we pulled a bonbon.

Since that time I have taught young Emma the way to play cards, and we also have a fine gramophone, with a fair number of good records. But although we had neither cards nor music at Christmas, nor on the day of our marriage, we certainly did not miss them. That young Emma could be happy under these conditions – a wedding without a honeymoon, and not even one friend to congratulate her – proved conclusively her fitness to be the wife of a shy and quiet man, who had always tried to shun the public eye.

CHAPTER XVI I

Solving the Mystery

IT WAS AN UNDERSTOOD thing between young Emma and myself, at this time, that there must be no sexual intercourse for the next six or eight weeks, in case my complaint was only sleeping and not dead. That our marriage could be happy under these conditions will appear strange to some people. But it must be remembered that we were going through the form of courtship, and nothing could be more pleasant than that; especially when we courted between the blankets, according to an old Welsh custom. This pleasant custom might have continued to the present day had it not been for certain men who were prophets – but not bards – sending up a loud cry that the land was being filled with bastards. But it seems a great pity that such a fine custom should have been discontinued because of a few accidents of that kind; and that we should be allowed to continue, in which such accidents are too common to mention. What was a shame in times of Peace seems to have been noble in times of War. But I must not begin to preach now, when I am almost at the end of my story; for I have tried to make this work simple and direct, with plenty of open space for the comments of others.

Young Emma and I were getting on very well, especially as we never parted company for more than an hour at a time, when I would take Beauty Boy for a short run in the green lanes. We had a few hasty words occasionally, but I could never understand how they came or why. These hasty words generally led to a few hours sulking in silence; after which we would recover our good humour as if nothing had happened. It was then that young Emma would tell me that she had bought something new – a dress, a hat or a pair of shoes. When this had happened several times, I came to the conclusion that it was not wise to quarrel with young Emma too often, unless I was ready with a spare pound or two in the bank. So that one day, when she had mentioned having seen a nice pair of shoes in a shop window, I asked her, with a sudden burst of enthusiasm – 'Would you like to have them?'

'That's the first time my Bunnykins has offered to buy me anything, without being asked for it,' she said – 'and I love him all the more for that.' The next moment she was dressed to go out, in case I should begin to count my money and advise a little delay.

There was one thing that young Emma could not understand, and that was my expenses in connection with the house itself, and that I had to be prepared to meet them. Although I did not thoroughly understand them myself, yet I knew they had to be paid. Young Emma suggested that the house should be made over to her, in her name, because no one would be so ungallant as to charge a *woman* rates or taxes of any kind. And when I told her it would make no difference, whether the house was owned by a woman or a man, she answered, with considerable emphasis – 'A collector of taxes is the last man in the world that I would think of marrying.'

It was now the twentieth morning of our marriage, and I went out for my usual walk with Beauty Boy, leaving young Emma in the kitchen, preparing the midday meal. 'We are quite happy as companion spirits,' thought I to myself, 'but as man and wife it is not altogether satisfactory and something must happen before long. The sooner it does, the better it will be for the both of us.'

It seemed strange that these thoughts should have come back to me, time after time, on this particular morning; for when I got back home I found young Emma lying on the couch and in great pain. However, the application of a hot-water bottle seemed to give her some relief and, before the evening came, she was much better.

'Do you know what caused the pain?' I asked.

'No,' she answered. 'I have had the same pains several times lately, but not so bad as today.'

Saying this she went on to describe her pains, and what parts of her body were affected by them.

'Emma,' I said – 'you have the same pains exactly as I had myself, and you must now see a doctor, even as I did. It is only fair to the both of us that you should do so without loss of time. Now, will you let me write a letter to my doctor, which you shall read, and post it to him this evening, to make an appointment for tomorrow?'

'But what are you going to say?' she asked, curious to know more.

'I am going to write the following words,' I said, 'to be sent on your approval.'

'Dear Doctor,

'My wife, who has been suffering lately with certain pains, is coming to see you tomorrow. Between ourselves, I believe she is suffering from a venereal complaint. But you will not get much information out of her, unless you ask her plenty of questions.'

'I don't like the idea of that letter,' protested young Emma, although she laughed at the last sentence – 'why not let the doctor find that out for himself?'

'Because,' I answered, quietly, 'a doctor requires a certain amount of information to begin with; otherwise he may not even suspect the real thing and treat his patient for something else. Sometimes a little information saves a lot of time and trouble. For instance, one day a man was knocked down by a heavy cart, which went over his right leg. While he was lying there helpless, surrounded by hysterical women who were holding their hands before their eyes in horror, and were making a great cry of "fetch a doctor" – while this was going on, that man suddenly sat up in the road and shouted in a savage, angry voice – "To hell with doctors – fetch a carpenter!" The man, you see, had a wooden leg, and could not stand or walk until it was repaired; otherwise he was not hurt. That will show you how far a little information will sometimes go, in saving time and emotion from being wasted.'

But although young Emma laughed again when she heard this, she still did not like the idea of sending that letter; in spite of my assertion that doctors thought nothing of such cases, and never talked to others, not even their own wives, of the complaints of their patients. Seeing this, I thought that perhaps a different kind of argument would bring me more success. So I began in this way – 'What do you think a woman once told me? She said that if I was a married man and became indifferent to sexual intercourse with my wife, she would look for it somewhere else.'

'But all wives are not like that,' answered young Emma quietly.

'When the husband is to blame, that may be so,' I said; 'but when the wife is to blame, it is quite common to find men who go, secretly, elsewhere for their gratification. Let me tell you a cold, hard fact, which is not generally known – a prostitute's principal customers are married men, and not single men, as is generally thought. If that were not the case, prostitutes, who are counted by the thousand, would be counted by the hundred. So that the great number of prostitutes is caused by their demand; and if married people did not starve each other sexually, more than two-thirds of our prostitutes would have to earn their living by honest work. You seem surprised to hear these things, and do not know why I mention them. Well, Emma, I will now ask you a question – 'Would you care much if I went after other women?'

When young Emma heard this, she was greatly alarmed, and looked serious indeed. In fact, there was one thing in her disposition which always gave me amusement, and that was her jealousy. On one occasion she was even jealous of an old skeleton of a woman with grey hair, and cried with vexation – without thinking of her own great advantages of youth and beauty. That she should be more jealous of me than I was of her, with all the advantage on her side, amused me considerably. When I received letters from women who admired my literary work, it always caused trouble.

Now, when I asked young Emma this question, if she would care much if I went after other women, it brought a very serious look into her face, as she said – 'But you would not do that without cause; and I am not going to give my Bunnykins the least cause to run after other women.'

'At present,' I assured her, 'there is not the least likelihood or inclination; but something must surely happen if this danger is not removed. You know very well that I have been afraid to co-habit since I received that fright before our marriage. If you do not see my doctor, and send him this letter, how can our present happiness continue?'

By this time young Emma had almost broken down, and I saw the same meek, pathetic look in her small, white face as I had seen before, when she was on the point of tears. Seeing this, I put my arms around her waist and kissed her, saying, at the same time – 'I don't want you to do anything against your will, but I wish you would take my advice in this matter.'

'Write the letter,' she said, impulsively, 'and I will post it immediately.'

As soon as young Emma had gone to the post, I was again tormented with doubt, in the same way as when I had caused the other letter to be written, when she was in the hospital. Again it seemed to me a cowardly attack on her character. However, in the present case, it was different; for if my doctor agreed with me, that my wife had a venereal complaint, he would certainly blame the husband, especially as I had already been under his care for the same trouble.

There was a great change now in young Emma's mood, from this time last night. Last night she was a child, full of strange ideas, but tonight she was a serious woman. Last night she had had the strange longing to see a baby elephant, and would talk of nothing else for more than an hour. She still mentioned it, even after I had told her a wonderful vision of my own; in which I saw the fattest lady on earth lifting the smallest man in the world, so as to kiss him beneath the mistletoe. What a strange and horrible change had come over us both during the last twenty-four hours!

When young Emma returned, after posting the letter, I tried to cheer her, but not with much success. Unfortunately I began, with every good intention, to say certain things that were not proper just then; for instead of making her more cheerful they only increased her sorrow. I began to say how much I studied her welfare and, if the worst came to the worst, she need have no fear of not being provided for. I told her that I would myself live a very plain and simple life, in order that she should not be in want, and that she would never have any trouble in getting me to keep my promises.

But while I was saying these things, I saw the same weak, suffering little face, silent and helpless, and I could say no more then. And when I put my arm around her, and sat with her on the couch, she broke down utterly, and sobbed so violently that I feared the strain on her heart. This lasted for several minutes, until my gentle stroking of her head and face made her so quiet that I thought she had cried herself to sleep, in the same way as children do. But she was thinking, and not sleeping; for it was not long before she said, in a small, meek voice – 'You are not going to leave me, Bunnykins, are you – no matter what the doctor says?'

'Of course I am not,' I answered cheerfully – 'we are too happy for that. The only reason you are seeing the doctor is because it will give our happiness a better chance to last.'

As I began to think, at this moment, that there was more danger in words than in music, I opened our gramophone, and we had a fine violin solo by a great master, followed by an old Elizabethan quartet by male voices. This music seemed to have a good effect on young Emma. So I lit my pipe and made myself look very happy in having tobacco, some music and her as a companion. In this way we spent the rest of the evening, until it was bedtime.

The next morning young Emma complained again of having pains, so I decided not to go out for my usual walk with Beauty Boy, in spite of his eagerness to rush into the street and take it by storm, leaving his anxious master to follow. In fact, I was more pleased than otherwise, to hear this news; for now I was certain that young Emma would not break her appointment with the doctor; which, if the pains had not returned, might have been the case. Now, although young Emma had read my letter to the doctor, it was intended that he should understand that I was making him a private communication, as the subject was too delicate to be discussed in her hearing. For that reason, I was not much surprised when, having seen him, she returned with only a bottle of medicine and a box of pills; but with no information, except that he was coming to see her in four or five days, after he had made a certain test.

'What did the doctor say, Emma ?' I asked, as soon as she had returned and settled down.

'He talked of wind, cramp, indigestion and constipation,' answered young Emma, 'and said that I needed plenty of exercise. And when I told him that I did all the housework myself, he said that that was not the kind of exercise I needed, but long country walks in the open air. After he had examined me, he said that he could find nothing wrong with my organs.'

'When he comes to see her in a few days' time,' thought I, 'he will probably tell her more than this. Or perhaps he is waiting to see me first, to answer me privately, in the same way as I am supposed to have communicated with him.'

The doctor was now making a test, and the result would be made known when he came at the end of the week. So there was nothing to do but to wait and use all my persuasive powers to coax young Emma to take her medicine. It seemed strange that I should be married to this child, who did not even have the courage to take a spoonful of medicine, and made ugly faces every time she thought of it.

CHAPTER XVIII

The End

YOUNG EMMA'S IGNORANCE OF venereal disease astonished me, as I have said before, for she did not seem to have any knowledge of its cause. She thought it was no more than some common ailment that was infectious; such as a cold that we could catch from each other if we kissed or breathed in each other's face. This was very fortunate for me in more ways than one; it not only saved her mind from a terrible anxiety, but it also enabled me to be more straightforward in expressing myself. This ignorance also prevented her from having any shame;otherwise she would not have posted my letter to the doctor, or made an appointment to see him, preferring to go to some strange doctor in another town, where she would not be known.

My little wife was a very bad patient, and it was with great difficulty that she could be persuaded to take medicine. As for taking long walks, she would not do this unless I accompanied her. It was no good to tell her that in my lonely country walks I got some ideas for my work, and that the presence of another would prevent them from coming. She could not understand this; nor could she understand me when I said our food, our clothes and shelter had to be paid for with my ideas, which needed a lonely hour or two to give them birth.

I had forgotten to say that the doctor had advised young Emma to get a dog for her country walks – a wolf-hound or a black retriever. This made her mention Beauty Boy, but the doctor said she ought to have one of her own, and leave Beauty Boy to his master. So that when young Emma came back, after her interview with the doctor, and said – 'May I have a dog, Bunnykins?' I, of course, said 'Yes'.

Well, the very next morning, in walked young Emma with a little tiny puppy in her arms; so small that it could sit in a tea plate and almost close its tail without falling over the rim. There could be no question of long walks now, for this little mite not only required a constant nurse, but also objected to being taken out into the open air. However, although this did nothing to help young Emma's body, it certainly gave a great pleasure to her affectionate spirit.

When the doctor came to see my wife, at the end of the week, I went into the garden, to leave them alone for a while. But before he left he came out to see me, as I had expected. 'The dog business is an utter failure,' he said with an amused smile. 'Now, what I want to see you about is this: it may be that your wife will need an operation, but I am not sure. For that reason, I would like her to see a good specialist, and I know the very man.'

'Very good,' I answered – 'perhaps you will make arrangements as soon as you can.'

'With regard to venereal disease,' continued the doctor, 'there is not only no sign of such a thing, but also nothing to show that she has had it.'

When I heard this I was astounded, and felt certain there was a mistake, although I said nothing against his opinion. 'We will hear what the specialist has to say,' thought I, 'before we believe that. It is certain that I got mine from a human body, and not from making love to a ghost or a shadow.'

The doctor lost no time in writing to his friend the specialist, and received an answer by return of post. The result was that young Emma had an appointment at the beginning of the following week. The idea of an operation alarmed her very much, but she said she would go through it for my sake – if I promised to sit at her bedside until she was better. On the day of her appointment with the specialist, young Emma went to London, accompanied by a lady friend, in case there was no nurse in attendance, and another woman would be needed. She would only be away a few hours, so I did not trouble about my own midday meal, and only fed the animals. I was very anxious to know the result, for I did not want the poor girl to have an operation, after what she had gone through in the hospital, before our marriage. However, if it was necessary, we would have to make the best of it.

At two o'clock, young Emma was back home, having been away no more than four hours; and the first words she uttered after our greeting, were – 'The specialist does not think an operation is necessary, and is going to write to the doctor to that effect.'

'Did he say anything about venereal disease,' I asked.

'Oh no,' answered young Emma, 'he said that all I needed were the same pills and medicine that the doctor is now prescribing, and plenty of outdoor exercise. He also said, the same as the doctor, that women do not drink enough, and I must drink three pints of liquid a day.' When I heard this, the whole truth came on me suddenly.

'You do not seem to be very pleased,' said young Emma, seeing my serious face.

The only answer I gave to this was to kiss her passionately, which gave her as much surprise as my first thoughtful expression. But I had plenty to think about, as soon as I could get a few minutes to myself.

That night, when I was lying quietly in bed, I went over the whole thing, from beginning to end; and the more I thought of it, the more horrible it became. For instance, if this poor girl, who was now sleeping at my side, had only realised the meaning of my charge against her, and my reproach, she would have left me long ago, that was certain. But instead of showing any ill temper or indignation, she had only shown me a meek, suffering little face, silent because it was all a mystery; and I had taken her silence to be her shame, her sorrow and her guilt.

It was strange that I never once suspected the real author of my trouble; that the woman with the silk stockings was the cause of it all. I had understood that a venereal disease showed itself within ten or fourteen days after intercourse, and it was nearly three weeks after my adventure with that woman, when I met young Emma and took her home with me. The question now came to this – did it not take a longer time to develop in my case, or did I fail to see it, becoming confident of being safe, after the first ten days' anxiety?

But the most horrible thought of all was this – how did young Emma escape infection? And if she had not – but at this thought I turned so violently in bed that young Emma, disturbed in her sleep, opened her eyes and asked with concern – 'Did you have a nightmare, Bunnykins?'

'Yes' I answered – 'and a most horrible one, too.'

This is the end of my story, told bluntly and honestly, and without exaggeration. For I have always been honest and sincere in my literary work, without thinking of popularity; and that, I suppose, is why I have remained poor. So that whoever buys this book is in no danger of stuffing a fat pig.

Appendix

THE LETTER TO JONATHAN CAPE, dated November 1924, in which George Bernard Shaw gave his reasons for advising against publication of *Young Emma*, is published here in full for the first time, with the kind permission of the Society of Authors on behalf of the Bernard Shaw Estate. The original is now part of a collection of historical and literary manuscripts at the Humanities Research Center of the University of Texas at Austin.

Very Private.
8th November 1924. 10 Adelphi Terrace, London W.C.2

Dear Mr Jonathan Cape,

I have read it. It is an amazing document, just like the old one: the same record of a fully developed, vigorous, courageous, imaginative, and specifically talented adult, with plenty of experience of civilized life in the best literary and other society in London, and with the outlook of a slum boy of six or seven.

I agree with you that its publication may do him harm, partly by classing him with the writers who are not *virginibus puerisque*, and partly by the revelation of the fact that the literary world of writers, publishers, editors and so forth, not to mention the people who have taken him up socially, are so completely alien to him as they were when he was a tramp. Also, what right has he to give away his wife?

If they were both dead it would be another matter: I am always in favour of publishing genuine documents, and would be sorry to see even Joyce's *Ulysses* suppressed. As it is, I should advise him not to publish it. But if you not only give him this advice but refuse to publish it for him he may go off to, say, Werner Laurie, who may undertake an edition of 2000 at 2 guineas, in his style of the Moore books, and give the author not only a substantial sum of money but copies enough to present to the few friends to whom he may possibly wish to make a sort of confession, so that they may not have any false pretences to reproach him with as to his domestic affairs.

I think therefore the decision must be left to himself.

As my wife wishes to read the book (I do not [t]hink he would object to this) I will, with your permission, keep it a day or two longer.

Faithfully
G. Bernard Shaw

Jonathan Cape Ltd.,
11 Gower Street,
W.C.1

Cicely Veronica Wedgwood (1910 – 1997) was an English historian who published under the name C. V. Wedgwood. She wrote biographies and narrative histories specializing in the history of 17th-century England and continental Europe. Her early career included employment as a reader for the publisher Jonathan Cape.

LIBRARY OF WALES

The Library of Wales is a Welsh Government project designed to ensure that all of the rich and extensive literature of Wales which has been written in English will now be made available to readers in and beyond Wales. Sustaining this wider literary heritage is understood by the Welsh Government to be a key component in creating and disseminating an ongoing sense of modern Welsh culture and history for the future Wales which is now emerging from contemporary society. Through these texts, until now unavailable or out-of-print or merely forgotten, the Library of Wales will bring back into play the voices and actions of the human experience that has made us, in all our complexity, a Welsh people.

The Library of Wales will include prose as well as poetry, essays as well as fiction, anthologies as well as memoirs, drama as well as journalism. It will complement the names and texts that are already in the public domain and seek to include the best of Welsh writing in English, as well as to showcase what has been unjustly neglected. No boundaries will limit the ambition of the Library of Wales to open up the borders that have denied some of our best writers a presence in a future Wales. The Library of Wales has been created with that Wales in mind: a young country not afraid to remember what it might yet become.

Dai Smith

LIBRARY OF WALES
FUNDED BY

Noddir gan
Lywodraeth Cymru
Sponsored by
Welsh Government

SERIES EDITOR: DAI SMITH

1	*So Long, Hector Bebb*	Ron Berry
2	*Border Country*	Raymond Williams
3	*The Dark Philosophers*	Gwyn Thomas
4	*Cwmardy*	Lewis Jones
5	*Country Dance*	Margiad Evans
6	*A Man's Estate*	Emyr Humphreys
7	*Home to an Empty House*	Alun Richards
8	*In the Green Tree*	Alun Lewis
9	*Ash on a Young Man's Sleeve*	Dannie Abse
10	*Poetry 1900–2000*	Ed. Meic Stephens
11	*Sport*	Ed. Gareth Williams
12	*The Withered Root*	Rhys Davies
13	*Rhapsody*	Dorothy Edwards
14	*Jampot Smith*	Jeremy Brooks
15	*The Voices of the Children*	George Ewart Evans
16	*I Sent a Letter to My Love*	Bernice Rubens
17	*Congratulate the Devil*	Howell Davies
18	*The Heyday in the Blood*	Geraint Goodwin
19	*The Alone to the Alone*	Gwyn Thomas
20	*The Caves of Alienation*	Stuart Evans
21	*A Rope of Vines*	Brenda Chamberlain
22	*Black Parade*	Jack Jones
23	*Dai Country*	Alun Richards
24	*The Valley, the City, the Village*	Glyn Jones
25	*The Great God Pan*	Arthur Machen
26	*The Hill of Dreams*	Arthur Machen
27	*The Battle to the Weak*	Hilda Vaughan
28	*Turf or Stone*	Margiad Evans
29	*Make Room for the Jester*	Stead Jones
30	*Goodbye, Twentieth Century*	Dannie Abse
31	*All Things Betray Thee*	Gwyn Thomas
32	*The Volunteers*	Raymond Williams
33	*Flame and Slag*	Ron Berry
34	*The Water-castle*	Brenda Chamberlain
35	*A Kingdom*	James Hanley
36	*The Autobiography of a Super-tramp*	W H Davies
37	*Story I*	Edited by Dai Smith
38	*Story II*	Edited by Dai Smith
39	*A Time to Laugh*	Rhys Davies
40	*Young Emma*	W H Davies
41	*We Live*	Lewis Jones
42	*Carwyn*	Alun Richards

WWW.THELIBRARYOFWALES.COM